BEYOND WILD

BEYOND WILD

GARDENS AND LANDSCAPES BY RAYMOND JUNGLES

INTRODUCTION BY MICHAEL VAN VALKENBURGH

EDITED BY AMANDA EVA JUNGLES

INTRODUCTION

MICHAEL VAN VALKENBURGH

I have loved Raymond Jungles's landscapes for a very long time. The way he amplifies daring compositions, in large part due to a profound appreciation of plants, has captured my imagination for years. His gardens are undoubtedly striking, but first and foremost they are comforting to visitors—a mirror of Raymond himself, a person who exudes quiet self-confidence and a sense of serenity. The same combination of tranquility and boldness is evident in the landscapes he admires, especially those designed by Roberto Burle Marx, an early and formative influence on his work. While both designers favor vivid colors and textures, it never feels like they are employed in the interest of drawing attention to themselves. On the contrary, judging by the completed gardens, both are interested in creating places for visitors simply to enjoy.

For many years I knew Raymond's work only through photographs. About ten years ago, I was able to experience his projects in person on a family vacation in Miami. The grandkids had a morning planned with their parents, so I called Raymond to ask for the addresses of a few sites to visit. He said he had a better idea, and within two hours we were cruising around in his convertible from one of his landscapes to another. The project that has stuck in my head ever since is a garden that goes along with a freestanding house on the roof of the Herzog & de Meuron–designed parking garage at 1111 Lincoln Road in Miami Beach.

When we reached the roof, I was pleasantly surprised by the elegance of the house that had been built on the top floor and the variety of spaces that flowed inside to out—and Raymond's masterful planting design. A roof garden has two qualities that landscape architects always struggle with: the relentlessly flat ground plane and the uninterrupted perimeter wall or railings. Raymond undoes the legibility of both, and in doing so turns a roof garden into something else: a true sky garden. He seizes on the upward sloping roof deck to dissolve the pavement and architecture into a skyward explosion of green. The gesture made me think of a more extravagantly scaled upward sweep at the far end of Vaux-le-Vicomte's grander central axis. But where André Le Nôtre interrupts the horizon beyond with a sculpture and brings everything to closure, Raymond builds to a crescendo of shrubs

and low trees before the landscape falls away to reveal boundless sky. Le Nôtre's axis is complete and resolute; Raymond's is open and free.

At some of the other edges on the roof, cascades of plants obscure the railed perimeter and free the garden from its containment. The role of these plants—to obscure a limiting edge—is crafted to form a series of fluid and unfolding outdoor spaces. In one area a skeletal wire trellis overhead is almost fully covered with the large-leaved native beach morning glory, adding further to the spatial complexity. It's a brilliant technique and a skillful part of one of the best gardens I have ever seen.

In his twenties Raymond spent time traveling with Burle Marx, and his influence is clear. One of my favorite examples is Raymond's recurring use of inventive pavement patterns in contrasting graphic bands of white and dark gray. This imparts a basic structure within the landscape, making clear with its rhythm that it is the result of human intervention. Yet as his abundant plantings spill into this simple geometry, the result is a dancing glimpse of order just in the moment of its surrender to joyful wildness.

Raymond knows an incredible array of plants—thousands probably—while also understanding each as a living thing with its own unique cultivation needs. This knowledge alone sets him apart from so many landscape architects who know precious little about plants and as a result outsource their planting designs. But what makes Raymond's work great is his skill in using plants as a design medium. He knows how to abstract them into artistic materials (hard to do with a living material) and playfully combines species from different natural ecologies to impart his intended feeling.

The rigor of Raymond's designs shows us that the traditional dichotomy of "formal" (geometric and clearly human-made) and "informal" (full of irregularity, as if a product of nature) is inadequate for describing contemporary landscape. I would never call Raymond's approach to planting "formal," but no one is a greater master of form in the medium of plants.

Raymond's signature is a particular kind of harmony, achieved by making gardens that are drawn from nature and at the same time fully the result of human artistry. His landscapes feel inevitable, but they are, in fact, the product of many approaches to planting design. One in particular is the carefully composed plant tableau: The opening photograph of this book is a fine example. I imagine Raymond taking special joy in how these tableau moments—the appearance, seemingly by chance but thoroughly intentional, of intensely charged relationships among a larger assemblage of plants—alter the rhythm of moving in his gardens. These small dramatic scenes are integral counterpoints to an encompassing, soft continuity that comforts us with lush thickets and reaching, twisting tendrils of green. To compose these, sometimes he may follow what may be called the French bouquet strategy of planting—using so many different species that no one dominates the others. Raymond's gardens at times push complexity to the brink—he is a genius at knowing how many different plants to add and where. And these define spaces that are open and serene: spaces where the absence of any plants dances back and forth with the groves and thickets and plant tapestries that may be nearby. Over the years his increasing use of native plants in these compositions has inserted tangible connections to site and, artistically, an appealing, scratchy coarseness to his work.

Certainly, Raymond is inspired by the natural world, but to say that he simulates nature misses the point entirely. Nature is not inherently generous. Raymond is. He composes landscapes with broad, confident gestures that come out of abundance. They are moments that are engulfing—places that hold you within a madness of plants. But his abundance always comes back to the same purpose: to make us feel good.

OPPOSITE AND PRECEDING PAGES: Sky Garden, Miami Beach.
ABOVE: Baker's Bay Garden.

THE MODERNIST GARDEN
NEW YORK BOTANICAL GARDEN

The Bronx, New York | 2019

The Modernist Garden had the honor of being the grand entrance to the New York Botanical Garden's largest botanical exhibition, *Brazilian Modern: The Living Art of Roberto Burle Marx.* The exhibition, at the edge of New York's concrete jungle, celebrated the life and legacy of the Brazilian modernist artist, landscape architect, and conservationist. Nearly 250,000 visitors experienced this horticultural tribute between June and October 2019.

The Conservatory Lawn, an unassuming grass expanse, was boldly transformed into a verdant nirvana and immersive experience for the senses. The Modernist Garden, with more than fifty species of predominantly tropical plants, displayed the exuberance of Brazilian modern through the lens of Jungles's lifelong admiration for Burle Marx.

The garden was installed in just two weeks; the timeframe was shortened by unusually cold temperatures in late May 2019. Many 35-foot-tall palms and specimen cycads, donated by Jungles and others, arrived safely in the Bronx on large semi-trucks that originated in Florida. Jungles utilized many of Burle Marx's favorite palm species, such as the *Copernicia baileyana* and *Attalea cohune*.

A serpentine black-and-white walkway guided visitors through a succession of garden moments and offered shaded canopies to pause and absorb interpretive signage that described Burle Marx and his design legacy.

Swaths of colorful groundcovers acted as focal points before the big reveal of a unique water feature interpretation of Burle Marx's mural at the Banco Safra building in São Paulo, Brazil. The sound of water filled the main space and acted as a soundtrack to the garden's centerpiece. Visitors happily congregated for events and enjoyed tranquil views in many of the pockets in and around the Modernist Garden.

Following Burle Marx's principles of creating beauty and community, the Modernist Garden was activated daily with public programming for all ages, including interactive samba lessons, Afro-Brazilian martial art, and Brazilian plant tours. It was also the highlight of the Garden's annual Conservatory Ball, hosting guests for the cocktail hour before dinner and dancing in the Conservatory Tent. The *Brazilian Modern* exhibition included an extensive group of Burle Marx's paintings, prints, drawings, and textiles. This material, installed in the Mertz Library, underscored the connection between his art and his environmental stewardship.

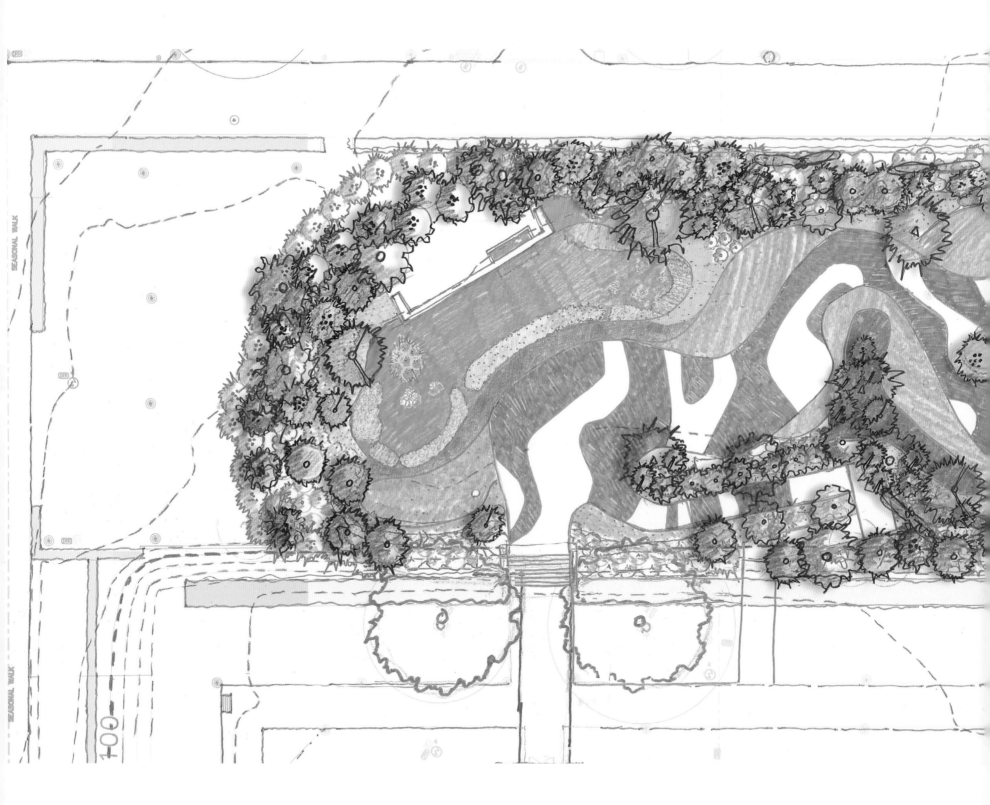

PRECEDING PAGES: Day- and night-blooming water lilies commingle with *Victoria cruziana, Victoria amazonica,* and *Victoria* 'Longwood Hybrid' in the water feature.

LEFT: The site plan reimagines the Conservatory Lawn as a botanical journey along a serpentine path.

ABOVE: A rendering anticipates the flow of visitors seen in the vista through the completed garden.

19

ABOVE: Roberto Burle Marx (1909–1994) was both an artist and a horticulturalist who explored Brazil's rainforest and cautioned the public early on about the damaging effects of deforestation.

RIGHT AND OVERLEAF: An aerial view of the visually captivating exhibition space that transformed the Conservatory Lawn. Burle Marx's love of plants, notably Brazilian plants, was legendary and contagious. Here a *Dypsis decaryi* or triangle palm, stands prominently in the center. Jungles first saw this palm at the Sítio Burle Marx in Rio de Janeiro.

PRECEDING PAGES: Massings of *Colocasia* 'Black Magic' soften the left and right sides of the water feature. The large bed of *Coleus* 'El Brighto' was grown by the horticultural staff at the New York Botanical Garden.

LEFT AND ABOVE: The focal point of the space is a sculptural mural inspired by Burle Marx's work at the Banco Safra headquarters. Jungles had watched Burle Marx create the original in São Paulo in 1983. Jungles's interpretation adds the sound and movement of water that both energizes and cools the space. Six specimen cycads, on loan from Jungles's private collection, have now returned to Florida, where they grow happily in his home garden in Coconut Grove.

Jungles celebrates the *Attalea cohune*, or American oil palm. The palm pictured here is just a baby. Mature palms can have a trunk as large as 36 inches in diameter with fronds more than 30 feet long. This is one of the largest-scaled palms and what Jungles would call a legacy palm. Burle Marx would use this palm as an anchor in his projects, clustered in groups of 5 to 7 or 11 to 15.

VISITOR CENTER GARDEN
NAPLES BOTANICAL GARDEN

Naples, Florida | 2014

In 2006 a collaborative team was formed by the Naples Botanical Garden to envision a master plan for 170 acres of land three miles south of downtown Naples. The plan that emerged encompassed a composition of gardens, to be constructed in phases, that has become the Naples Botanical Garden we see today. Construction began in 2008 on several gardens, including the Children's Garden, the Caribbean Garden, and the Brazilian Garden, and with the opening of the Visitor Center Garden in 2014, the initial phase of the project was complete.

While the Visitor Center Garden stands out on its own as the heart of the overall master plan and the hub of activities, the garden was always in the minds of the designers who conceived the surrounding gardens as well. For instance, the Brazilian Garden, also designed by Jungles, sits as the visual focal point from the "Prow" at the terminus of the Visitor Center Entry Pavilion. Standing there, visitors are fully immersed in the surrounding gardens, with a direct view of the cascading water feature and vivid mural by Roberto Burle Marx within the Brazilian Garden beyond.

Upon arriving at the Visitor Center Garden, patrons enter through a lushly planted threshold that leads to a boardwalk meandering through dense vegetation. The arrival and ticketing buildings, which appear to float above the land, are scaled as a backdrop to the larger landscape. The program is broken down into a series of smaller buildings to allow visitors the opportunity to continually engage the botanically diverse natural habitats. The garden and architecture exist symbiotically; as the trellis-like buildings host vines, the garden supports the gently placed volumes.

The garden continues a legacy of preservation by engaging the surrounding local ecosystems in an environmentally responsible way. The seven wooden pavilions, designed by the Texas architects Lake | Flato, were crafted from local and durable "sinker" cypress and are entwined throughout the gardens and various plant collections to create an immersive and engaging experience for visitors and researchers as well as an enticing venue for large events. The buildings and pavilions received LEED Gold certification through the U.S. Green Building Council.

Water links the spaces throughout the entire garden through a series of streams, water gardens, ponds, and lakes. From the arrival area, water trickles over native stone boulders into a water garden nestled adjacent to the ticketing booth. This pond provides a reflection of the tropical foliage and the warm wood accents of the minimal yet striking architecture. The garden's spine, a flowing corridor of aquatic plants, leads visitors and water alike toward the great lawn and down the "River of Grass." The figurative and literal River of Grass alludes to the Everglades—South Florida's most dominant landscape feature—while filtering stormwater at the heart of the garden. This River of Grass establishes itself at the Visitor Center Garden and flows throughout the site, creating a living ribbon that unites and enlivens the overall master plan.

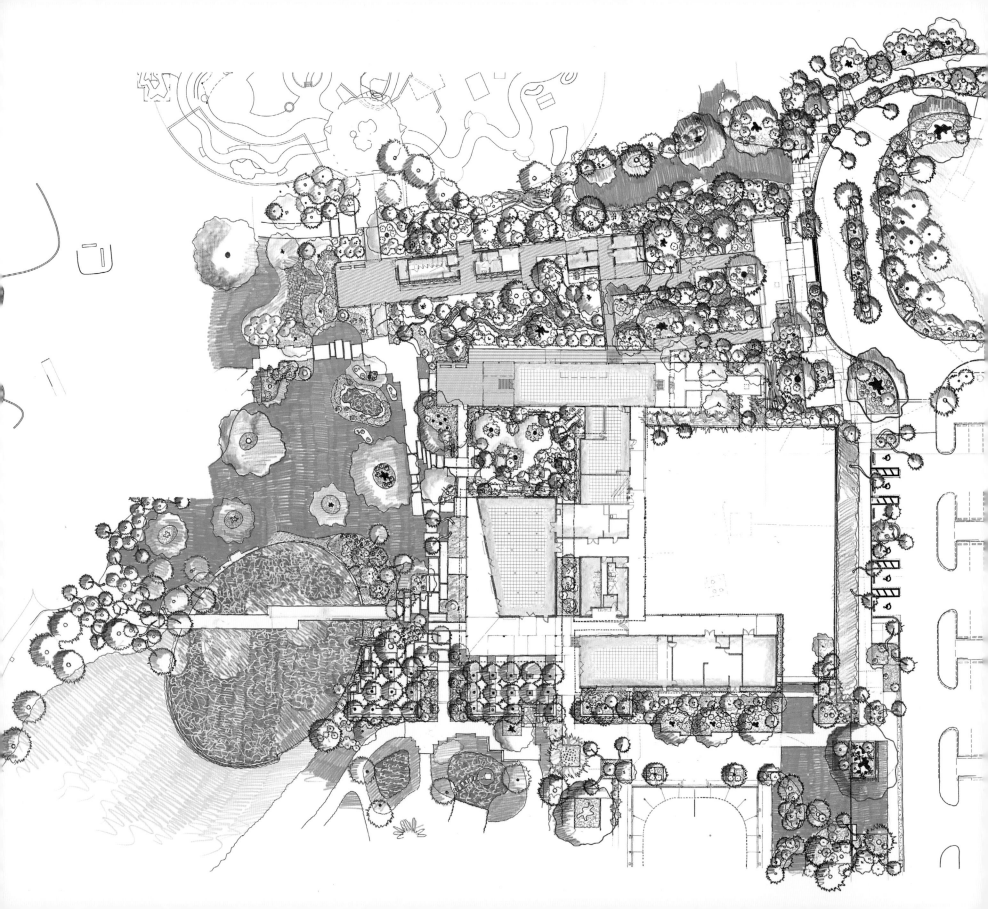

The visitor center complex, 14,000 square feet of interior space, houses the various functions for ticketing, retail, exhibit, conference, and cafe/dining. All circulation is exterior with trellis covered pathways and shaded gathering areas. Views from each of the interior spaces feature dramatic vignettes of specimen trees, carefully placed water features, and unique moments of vegetative ingenuity. The interweaving of interior and exterior spaces creates a dynamic and ever-changing experience for guests.

At the heart of the complex is the LaGrippe Orchid Garden. This intimate courtyard space features a myriad of colorful and fragrant orchid species and cultivars from around the globe. On display are orchids ranging from dainty, leafless plants with inconspicuous green flowers, to plants with giant, showy blossoms that perfume the air. Featured alongside orchids are some of the garden's large collections of bromeliads and other epiphytes growing in the canopies of the trees. The rough bark of the silver trumpet tree provides a natural armature for air plants while providing dappled shade and bursts of bright yellow color each spring. Limestone boulders, native to south Florida, are carved into troughs for cascading water to spill over, providing serene sounds found in the wild and allowing visitors to be immersed in the tranquil nature of the garden.

The Naples community was integral in making the dream of this garden become a reality. While the master plan was a major collaboration of talented designers, none of it would have been possible without the community's support and participation. Several large donations of prized botanical specimens were given to the garden by local plant societies to contribute to the overall success of the project. The Naples Botanical Garden staff self-performed the plant installation with the guidance of Jungles and his team. The entire project was a labor of love for the entire Naples community and all involved.

PRECEDING PAGES: Arriving visitors follow an intimate walkway that meanders through the dense vegetation. The arrival and ticketing buildings are scaled as a backdrop to the larger landscape.

LEFT: The site plan emphasizes the interior and exterior integrations proposed by both Jungles and Lake | Flato Architects.

ABOVE: A watercolor sketch of the proposed LaGrippe Orchid Garden developed for fundraising efforts. This intimate courtyard space features a myriad of colorful and fragrant orchid species and cultivars from around the globe.

LEFT: The siding of the Visitor Center is sawn from the reclaimed heartwood of ancient sinker cypress logs from the Apalachicola River. When Lake | Flato submitted the project for an AIA award, the jury questioned whether the landscape was inserted into a building or the building was inserted into the landscape.

RIGHT: An oolite water feature at the entrance to the garden.

OVERLEAF: From the Prow designed by Lake | Flato, guests of all ages are fully immersed within the tropical foliage while enjoying views directly across to the cascading water feature and the vivid Burle Marx mosaic mural in the adjacent Brazilian Garden.

LEFT: A performance lawn was integral to the overall master plan, and it is used regularly for events. The Prow beyond blends seamlessly with the dense vegetation and provides a dramatic relationship with the lawn for hosting groups of various sizes and functions.

OPPOSITE: View from the Brazilian Garden back toward the Prow at the Visitor Center.

FLORIDA GARDEN
NAPLES BOTANICAL GARDEN

Naples, Florida | 2017

For the reconfiguration of the Florida Garden, Jungles conceptualized the garden's untapped potential by visually expanding the original one-acre area to include the offsite views of the untouched natural Florida landscape, Lake Tupke and Deep Lake, and the wildlife that thrive within these elements. It is not unusual to spot tarpon and blue crab in the water and coyotes, bobcats, panthers, and bears in the surrounding preserve.

Supported by donors Karen and Robert Scott, the project focused on raising the entire site to provide a variety of garden experiences with a maximum 5 percent slope and a circulation system that contours through parts of the garden.

Of particular concern were two smaller areas within the overall garden, the Ideas Garden and the Sensory Garden, that were difficult to find. Jungles rerouted some of the circulation paths to further define an entrance between the two gardens. He created landforms of ten-foot-tall oolite monoliths on either side to compress the entrance and carved the tops for planters of epiphytes and cascading vines. As visitors enter through this compression, the garden slopes downhill, presenting a long vista to one of the lakes. Then the path winds fourteen feet uphill to two Chickee huts that serve as event space for weddings and outdoor programming. These shelters, made of palmetto thatch over a cypress log frame, were built by Florida's Big Cypress Seminole Indian Tribe.

The Naples Botanical Garden staff wanted the Florida Garden to be more inclusive of other plants that Jungles used in his gardens, perhaps a bit more theatrical than a native-only plant palette. The result is a combination of botanical specimens within a foundation of peripheral native plantings. Groundcovers include grasses and wildflowers—a mini "river of grass."

Jungles worked with the staff and water garden guru Mark Massey in setting large capstone boulders within the main water element. Water recirculates from the lakes to the upper pond. Gravity lends a hand in leading it back to the lake through various waterfall cascades and stream elements.

Naples itself is home to a committed group of plant collectors. Many specimen palms were donated from garden member collections including *Copernicia* palms from Cuba, flowering yellow *Tabebuia* trees from Brazil, and many others were rescued by staff from nearby construction sites.

PRECEDING PAGES: Phoenix palms and *Copernicia baileyana* are reflected in the dark surface of the lower water basin. Florida capstone boulders were artfully arranged for a tiered auditory experience.

OPPOSITE: The composite site plan shows the way the water elements link to the natural bodies of water, visually enlarging the garden for visitors meandering through.

RIGHT: Watercolor sketches of the water feature and entry were developed for fundraising efforts.

43

OPPOSITE AND ABOVE: In front of the Chickee hut, a water cascade flows from the upper basin into the lower water garden. Jungles brought the adjacent landscape in to make the entire river of grass, wetlands, bird sanctuary, lake, and natural ecosystem beyond all work together to reflect Florida's natural beauty.

Native Florida wildflowers enhance the path to the neighboring lake and line the edges of the stream that trickles down from the water garden. Views of the larger landscape integrate the Florida Garden into the plan for the Naples Botanical Garden as a whole.

GROVE STUDIO GARDEN

Grove Studio, at the intersection of Aviation and 27th Avenues, is the office of Raymond Jungles, Inc. The garden envelops a renovated building and extends into the public right-of-way along 27th Avenue. As a new variant of civic space, Grove Studio immerses its employees as well as Miami residents in the botanical richness and beauty of South Florida. The studio embodies the design principles Jungles has brought to tropical and subtropical gardens for more than thirty-five years: simplicity, timelessness, and biodiversity.

Located within walking distance from the Coconut Grove metro station, the three-story building was designed in 1981 by a local architect and then fully restored in 2018 by Jungles. The planting design is not confined to the property lines. Rather, it spills out of the half-acre lot and into the surrounding public right-of-way, establishing a verdant gateway into the heart of Coconut Grove and evoking a natural, preexisting tonality. Dense thickets of trees and shrubs showcase the wild and verdurous character of the area that had disappeared from this heavily trafficked corridor. Building on the city's recent improvements to the avenue, Grove Studio provides improved pedestrian circulation, shade, and botanical interest.

The garden and interior space foster a creative and dynamic work environment for the Jungles team of landscape architects and designers. Within the building, open floorplans and large windows allow nearly panoramic glimpses into the surrounding canopy. The garden is a diverse planting of native greenery composed of more than 124 species. Elegant concrete paving replaced the cracked asphalt parking lot. A naturalistic water feature houses aquatic flora and fauna; the waterfall delivers an ambient sound that cascades throughout the ground floor and provides a respite outside of the office for the staff. The ground floor and garden also serve as an outdoor gathering space, a perfect spot that helps to express the studio's culture, often frequented for ping pong, yoga, or outdoor lunches. Protected bike racks and a covered outdoor shower encourage staff to utilize the nearby metro station and newly installed bike paths, invoking a sustainable studio culture invested in lowering its carbon footprint and absorbing the natural environment.

Coral rock walls, monolithic oolite stone planters, and architectural fencing borders the property and seamlessly integrates with the encircling landscape. The oolite basin and monoliths were

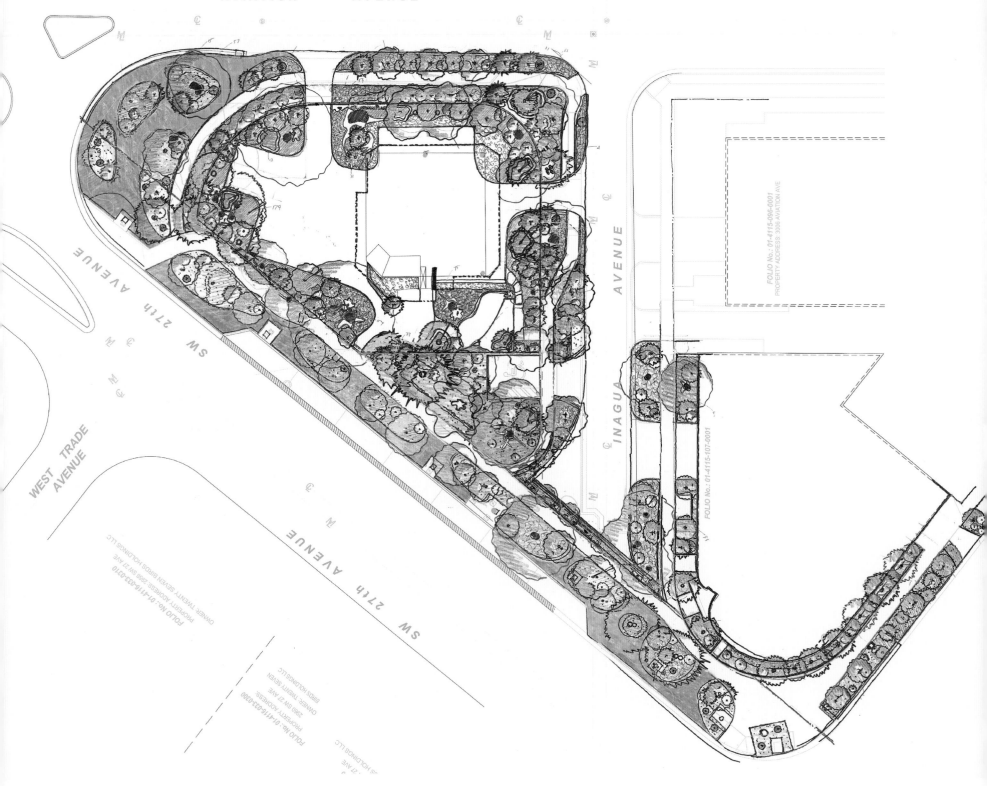

SW 27th AVENUE

WEST TRADE AVENUE

SW 27th AVENUE

INAGUA AVENUE

FOLIO No.: 01-4115-096-0001
PROPERTY ADDRESS: 3006 AVIATION AVE

FOLIO No.: 01-4115-107-0001

FOLIO No.: 01-4116-033-0310
PROPERTY ADDRESS: 2988 SW 27 AVE
OWNER: TWENTY SEVEN BIRDS HOLDINGS LLC

FOLIO No.: 01-4116-033-0200
PROPERTY ADDRESS: 2980 SW 27 AVE
OWNER: TWENTY SEVEN BIRDS HOLDINGS LLC

PRECEDING PAGES: The studio is like a tree house: each floor offers a different view of the garden from understory to canopy. In the mornings, squirrels bounce from limb to limb of the moss-covered *Quercus virginiana.* After a hard rain, a chorus of frogs fills the air.

OPPOSITE: The site plan shows the garden's generous extension into the right-of-way and public areas of the neighboring apartment complex.

ABOVE: Renderings show the impact the landscape would have from the street.

OVERLEAF: Dense planting envelopes the building, as seen from above, and offers a shady respite for pedestrians and habitat for birds and butterflies, including the rare Atala butterfly. A Baobab tree, salvaged from demolition after Hurricane Irma, was moved to the site.

quarried from beneath the parking lot and used as dramatic features carefully interspersed throughout the garden as planters or sculpture.

A similar yet unique balance between architecture and nature is found on each level of the building. On the second and fourth floors, the two design studios share remodeled interiors that have views into the garden through the limbs of a specimen live oak, gumbo limbos, sabal palms, thatch palms, and banana leaves that sway in the wind. On the third story, which serves as both an open conference and office space for Jungles and his wife, Gina, floor-to-ceiling glass windows and doors create a treehouse atmosphere. On all stories, oak trees with resurrection ferns burst to life after a rainstorm. The open floorplan and sculptural limbs of live oak trees and legacy kapok trees allow visitors to witness the passing of time and change of season.

Kapok trees and character sabal palms complement the height and form of the facade of the building. At different times throughout the day, light passes through tall branches and paints abstract shadows onto the surface.

The Studio Garden is a living gallery of Jungles's art—from sculptural trees to sculptural artwork including *Testigos* by Colombian sculptor Hugo Zapata. Custom oolite planters were quarried from below the parking court. In their place, an infiltration trench percolates all rainwater.

OPPOSITE: The garden is an amalgamation of textures, colors, and growth habits of plant material. Clockwise from upper left: Branches of a kapok tree are projected onto the facade; roots become poetic gestures from above; a specimen *Pachira aquatica* tree thrives in the lower water table of the public realm landscape.

RIGHT: A new auxiliary building, designed to house equipment, material samples, and a shower area, doubles as a water feature that brings a pleasant sound of falling water (and frogs) to passersby. The green roof features specimen cycads and aquatic plants.

LEFT: The tree house effect is evident on all the studio floors. Here, the third-floor balcony overlooks the sprawling limbs of a live oak tree, *Quercus virginiana*.

ABOVE: A schematic plan by Roberto Burle Marx is draped across the drawing board and provides daily inspiration to all.

OVERLEAF: Neighbors from all directions frequent this block to walk their dogs and bike with their children. The palm canopies and understory shrubs soften the public right-of-way and provide botanical interest day and night.

GROVE AT GRAND BAY GARDEN

Coconut Grove, Florida | 2014

Jungles's vision for the Grove at Grand Bay was to seamlessly meld its gardens with the historic village community of Coconut Grove and the dynamic towers designed by Bjarke Ingels Group (BIG). Timeless elegance informed the material choices, and the garden appears to have always been there.

Coconut Grove, or "The Grove," as locals call it, has been a haven for writers, artists, thinkers, and iconoclasts for more than one hundred years, and it is the oldest neighborhood in Miami. In 2011 Jungles accepted the challenge to "re-grove the Grove" on this prominent site.

In collaboration with a talented client and consultant team, Jungles led many major design moves including conceptualizing the vehicular and pedestrian circulation through the entire site. All the topographical lines are curvilinear at the perimeter, becoming straight as they approach the towers. Similarly, the natural oolite stone changes from a raw porous finish to a more honed surface. Large legacy trees on the site provide immense areas of shade. Curving forms, gracious ramps, and twisting palm trees complement the spiraling geometry of the 20-story residential towers. With floor plates that rotate every three feet at every elevation from the 3rd to the 17th floor, the gracefully twisting towers appear to float over the lush, canopied oasis and turn to capture the view as they rise to the sky. Ingels designed the towers to "dance together, to create space for each other, yet respond to each other and the environment."

Views down into the gardens, toward the surrounding canopied neighborhoods, and beyond to Sailboat Bay offer peaceful, verdant backdrops to residential units with vast balconies. From any point and at any garden level, one may look up towards the sky to see two amazing pieces of sculpture that guide the eye up toward the clouds.

Visitors arriving by car pass through an oolite guardhouse into the porte-cochère area, which is covered by a spiraling concrete canopy known as "the ribbon." Limited planting depths on the roof support a unique palette of resilient and cascading groundcovers that create an intriguing garden view from above.

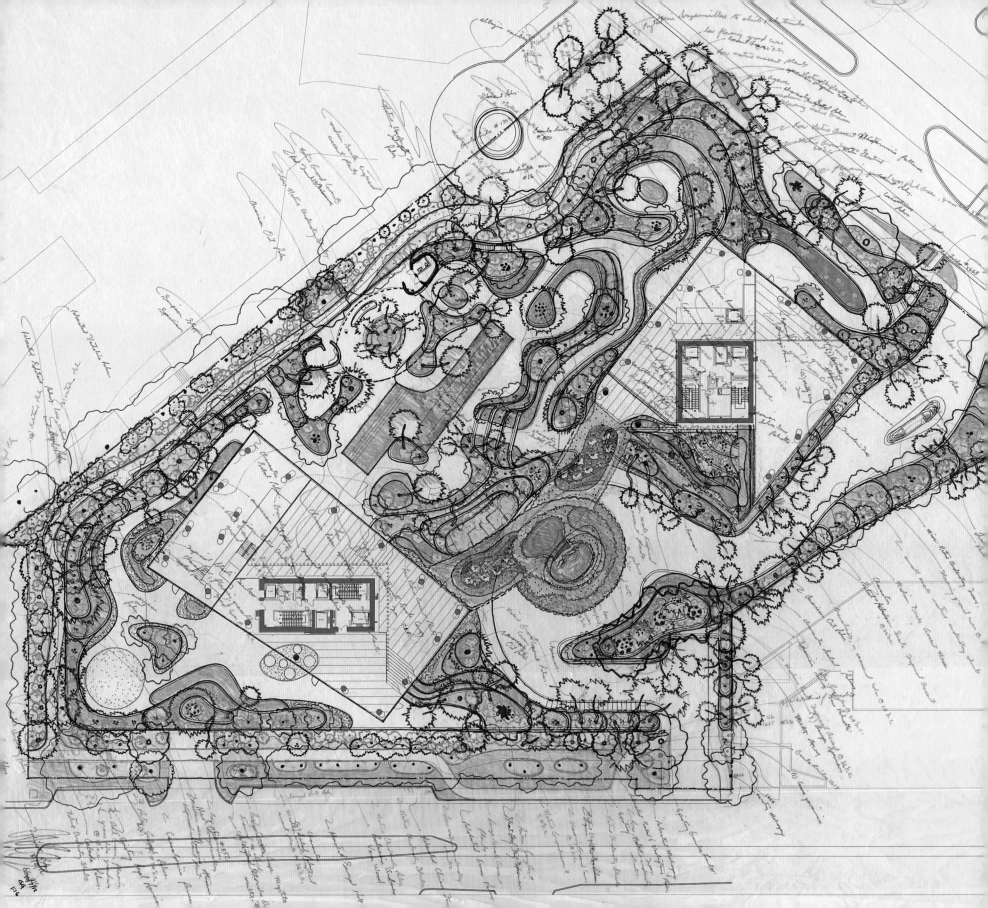

PRECEDING PAGES: Native quarried limestone was used for the pool deck and throughout the garden to create a timeless elegance while further embracing inside-outside continuity.

LEFT: Handwritten notations on the composite site plan reveal Jungles's process for specifying plant material.

ABOVE: Aerial view of the Grove at Grand Bay and the adjacent Regatta Park and Sailboat Bay. The derelict Grand Bay Hotel was demolished to make way for this iconic residential project with twisting towers and a feast of garden spaces.

OVERLEAF: "The ribbon" ties the two towers together and incorporates a green roof that can be appreciated from above. Plantings were appropriately selected for the limited soil depths of the green roof.

The south tower welcomes pedestrians with an oolitic rock multi-tiered garden that incorporates a tranquil water element that neutralizes traffic noise from adjacent Bayshore Drive and creates a feeling of serenity on the path to the lobby. This public space offers Grove residents a pocket of respite during their strolls in the neighborhood.

The gardens were designed to encompass a range of interests, with shade structures, secluded areas for contemplation, water gardens, and communal gardens. To minimize the significant grade change of the site, Jungles carefully designed the circulation to achieve slopes no greater than 5 percent.

The project utilized more than 470 canopy, understory, and palm trees and more 15,400 plants, more than 75 percent native, the largest amount of plant material and species to be incorporated in a commercial development in the area.

The overall result is a lushly landscaped campus that echoes the natural aura of Coconut Grove and promotes sustainability, with the Grove at Grand Bay as the first all-residential tower to achieve LEED Gold status in Miami. The project and corresponding gardens have brought tremendous attention to Coconut Grove, further defining a level of quality for future developments in the Miami area.

Installation of the gardens has acted as a catalyst, sparking conversation about future landscape improvements throughout the neighborhood. Uplifting and iconic, the gardens at the Grove at Grand Bay enhance the village experience, graciously shading the ample public and pedestrian experiences with park-like amenities.

Jungles's home and design studio are in Coconut Grove, so his involvement with the project's development was personal and is part of his firm's daily experience.

PRECEDING PAGES: Both towers twist, responding to the surroundings and to each other, giving optimum views of the lush pool area and other amenity spaces. Private balconies overlook the pool, spa, and a series of outdoor pocket "rooms" shaped by the geometry of the raised planters.

LEFT: Crooked *Sabal palmetto* shoot through the pool pavilion, creating a lively pattern in the sky.

BELOW: A secluded lounging pavilion can be covered and enclosed with fabric shades.

OPPOSITE AND LEFT: The spa is an intimate space within the garden for residents. The organic flow of the landscape complements the geometry of the architecture.

ABOVE: The functional area serving the parking garage was transformed into a multi-level garden element.

RIGHT: The water garden is part of the public realm, a gesture for neighborhood enjoyment.

ZEN DEN GARDEN

Jungles first walked the project site many years ago when it was owned by an orchid aficionado and patron of the Fairchild Tropical Botanic Garden. It is a spectacular property, rich in mature, multi-branched oak trees adorned with orchids and epiphytes. The 2.9-acre site boasts more than 400 feet of lakefront on one of the finger lakes in the Snapper Creek Lakes community in Miami.

The architect, Cesar Molina, is both a good friend and frequent collaborator. He contacted Jungles about the project, noting the clients' admiration of the gardens he had designed for two of their brothers and respective families.

As part of a design team with many years of experience working together, Jungles focused on the schematic and design development phases, creating bold moves in grading, hardscape, and planting. The result is a garden and a house that speak the same language.

Zen Den was influenced by the clients' affinity for the open-air pavilions, placid water gardens, and reflective ponds of the Amanyara in the Turks and Caicos. The garden design focused on configuring the topography to maximize the connection to the water's edge while protecting and elevating the presence of the three dozen mature oak trees that have long called this land home.

To bring the front garden motor court to the ideal elevation, Jungles excavated four to five feet of earth and lowered existing oak trees accordingly. A few oaks tower above the rest, as they remain at their original grade, reinforced with locally sourced oolitic limestone monoliths as retention walls. The driveway's dark concrete pavers, our "native stone" in Florida, mask the inevitable oak stains and tire tracks to come. The pavers were designed at a human-scale to prevent cracking from unstable grades and ground settling.

Committed to saving as many existing trees as possible, Jungles successfully relocated five specimen oak trees to allow for the architectural interventions. The periphery of the property is planted primarily with indigenous species for sustainability; close to the house there is an emphasis on plant selection for tropical texture and botanical interest—a veritable botanical garden.

Along the length of the property, bold branches of oak trees frame views towards multiple destinations within the garden. A focal point is the "spider oak" with its long, fern-laced branches that weep down and curve back up, mimicking a spider's legs, celebrated in the view from the principal bedroom.

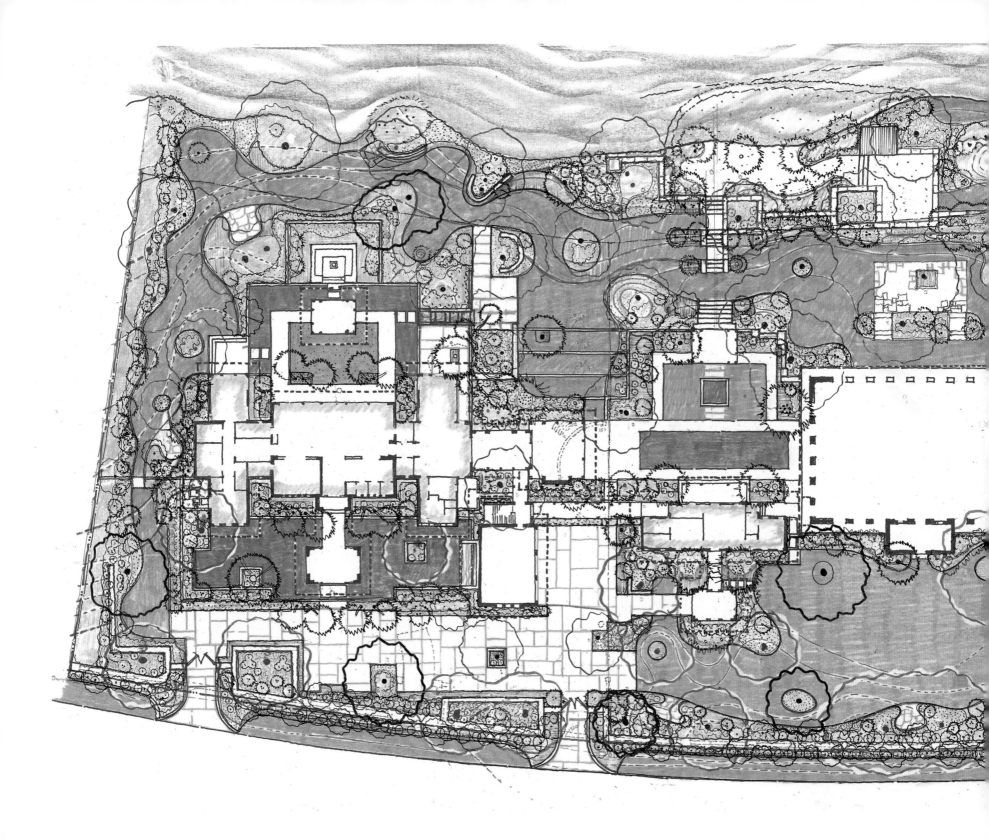

PRECEDING PAGES: The ipe terrace is accentuated by specimen *Satakentia liukiuensis* palms.

LEFT: Existing oak trees, many relocated to more opportune areas for celebration of their stature, are notated in faint blue canopy outlines on the site plan.

TOP: A specimen *Quercus virginiana* and *Corypha umbraculifera* frame the covered entry loggia.

RIGHT: The clients were inspired by the architecture and gardens of the Amanyara in the Turks and Caicos.

There are shaded, meditative places as well as large expanses of lawn for entertaining. A secluded beach area is ideal for kayak launching before or after an impromptu ping-pong match. The garden's ambiance shifts in the evening as the light from the fire pit dances on the built-in seating area and entertainment pavilion beyond.

Every project has a "sweet spot," where the views are paramount, be it the sky, water, distant architecture, or mountains. For Zen Den, the sweet spot is immediately adjacent to the beach. Jungles created a deck that cantilevers out over the water's edge. From that vantage point, the eye follows the entirety of the finger lake and tricks the mind into believing that you are in the primal wilderness.

The spa and lakeview pavilion are framed by limbs of giant oak trees adorned with bromeliads and orchids. A built-in lounge floats above the shallow entry point.

This water garden and entertainment terrace are elevated almost four feet above the ground level to maximize views and to create more interesting site topography.

OPPOSITE AND ABOVE: The open-air pool pavilion is perfect for entertaining. The green leaves of *Heliconia rostrata* grow adjacent to beautifully louvered wood panels.

OVERLEAF: The giant limbs of specimen oak trees, where epiphytic plant life is thriving, form an imposing arc over the expansive lawn areas designed to accommodate 500-person fundraising events.

Zen Den is based on garden moments and time spent moving through them.
A cantilevered seating area at the edge of the lake (opposite above) is Jungles's
favorite spot on the property. Friends gather to savor views across the water and
expanse of the lakeside garden. The beach area (opposite below) is accentuated
with pops of *Muhlenbergia capillaris* and swaths of *Microsorum scolopendrium*.

The built-in fire pit area aligns with Cesar Molina's architecture.
Philodendron 'Burle Marx' and *Alcantarea imperialis* offer various shades
of green surrounding the lawn.

PINE TREE NORTH GARDEN

The exterior design of this house demonstrates how garden elements can meld the built environment seamlessly with the natural. The family compound has a continuous design language, from the site-specific use of materials to the indigenous plantings and specimen trees. Jungles's design is natural and lush, and plant species were composed to create a wild feel. In addition to a linear saltwater swimming pool, the garden features a 100-foot long bio-filtered natural swimming pool or lagoon where red mangrove and native wetland plants thrive.

At the street end of the long, narrow lot a separate multifunctional pavilion, used for entertaining, sports, and exhibitions, ensures the privacy of the main house. Along the perimeter, large-scale sabal palms screen the neighboring structures.

The architecture incorporates raw materials such as exposed concrete, stone, and wood to complement the natural site. A curvilinear walkway supported on concrete stilts becomes a bridge over the natural pool and leads to the main living area on the second floor. From this vantage point, there are expansive views to the vegetated green roof of the bedroom wing below and out to Indian Creek and the Miami Beach skyline. A wall of sliding glass doors opens to the terrace, which is bookended by wooden walls and fronted by a glass balustrade. From here, it is possible to see Collins Avenue and the Eden Rock and Fontainebleau hotels.

The concrete driveway and pathways incorporate a finish of exposed shells that were sourced regionally in Florida. Joints notched out of the concrete were planted with sod to create permeable areas and to meld the hardscape and softscape together.

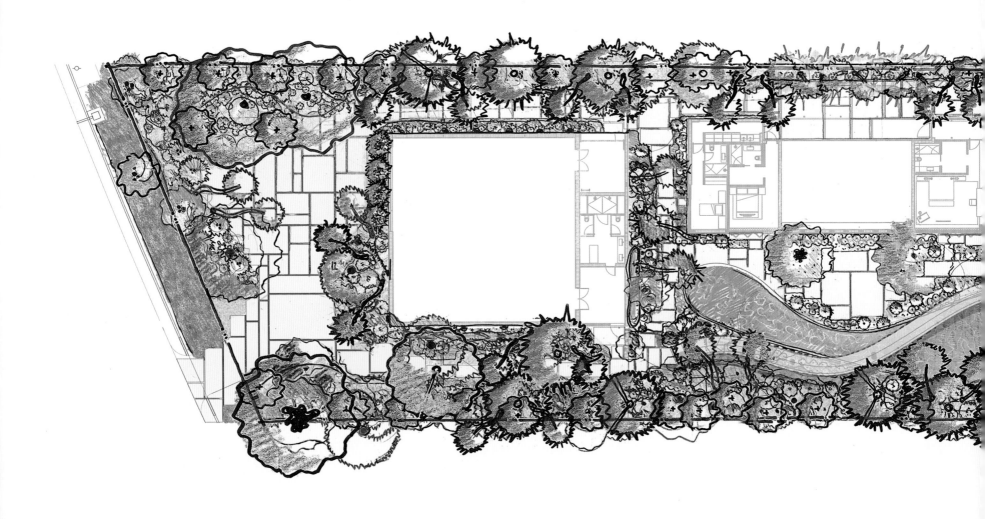

PRECEDING PAGES: Concrete stilts anchor the snake-like path and teak slats of the pedestrian entry bridge. The bio-filtered natural swimming pool below includes red mangrove and native wetland plants.

ABOVE: The site is on Pine Tree Drive, the strip of land that fronts Indian Creek. Like other properties on this stretch, the building is positioned to the rear of the site to capitalize on water views. Jungles provided landscape and hardscape design and collaborated with Studio MK27 on the elevated walkway and swimming pools.

The gradual rise of the elevated walkway provides a variety of perspectives and experiences of the courtyard garden. The path leads to the main living space on the upper level of the house.

Exterior spaces act as extensions of the interior rooms. A *Pithecellobium tortum* is aglow with the morning sunlight. The concrete pathway incorporates a finish of exposed shells that were sourced regionally in Florida. The integration of the lush planting softens the edges of the hardscape elements in the garden.

OPPOSITE: Large-scale, twisting sabal palms and other trees block the view of the neighboring house and bring a native Florida feel to the garden. Jungles extended Studio MK27's concept of a simple green roof by incorporating flowering bromeliads that can be seen from above and below.

ABOVE: The wood scrim facade opens to the natural swimming pool.

The reflection in the swimming pool reveals the seamless connection between the architecture and the landscape. The balcony offers stunning views of Miami Beach's art deco skyline.

JADE SIGNATURE GARDEN

Following their successful collaboration on 1111 Lincoln Road and the Sky Garden, Herzog & de Meuron invited Jungles to design the gardens for Jade Signature, a 57-story concrete tower intended to "evoke the relationship to nature and the environment that has long made Miami such a unique destination."

Despite the fact that 90 percent of the garden is built on top of structure, the tower appears to emerge from the landscape, with the beach on one side and forest on the other. Resident parking is underground rather than in a podium at the base of the tower, allowing Jungles to conceptualize a seamless garden experience from street to shore and to make it look like it was all on natural earth.

A ribbon-like concrete driveway takes cars from Collins Avenue up to the drop-off entrance on the west side. Jungles thought it fitting to procure a 60-foot specimen kapok tree to grow up through the tree well of the circular ramp. It was craned into the space and quickly flushed its leaves. The kapok's buttress roots and branching character provide sculptural punctuation visible from all heights and angles.

The parallelogram footprint of the tower maximizes the pool and beach exposure to the sun and allows the southern sun to have an extended presence on the beachside landscape. A colorful range of botanically rich native coastal vegetation gives the Dune Garden a relaxed, distinctly Floridian character. Sea grape, sculptural buttonwoods, and seven-year apple, along with swaying coconut and sabal palms, create pleasant pockets of shade, while natural grasses and carpets of indigenous wildflowers encircle the dune landscape. Canopies of mature trees provide opportunities for quiet moments of relaxation, and on the leeward side, shelter for residents and passersby equally.

The Pool Garden is a natural extension of the Dune Garden. The gentle lines and organic forms of the lagoon pool and planting areas meld with the beach. Whether lounging in a hammock or from cleverly positioned, comfortable furniture, a variety of garden experiences and great views abound.

Countless reflections of the garden, ocean, and architecture play across the generous surface of the lagoon pool. The lap pool zone delivers views into the Leeward Garden from a more intimate, sunny vantage point while offering ample opportunities for open-air exercise. The Leeward Garden, sheltered by the architecture, is a verdant oasis in the town of Sunny Isles.

The volumes created by canopy trees are juxtaposed with the staggered heights of coconut, sabal, and date palms, creating a living, ever-changing work of art. Florida silver palms, native *Lignum vitae*, green, and key thatch palms comprise the understory layer of the garden adding depth and texture to this composition. While in unity with its urban context, the garden is distinctly lush and appears to be preexistent, as if it had always been there.

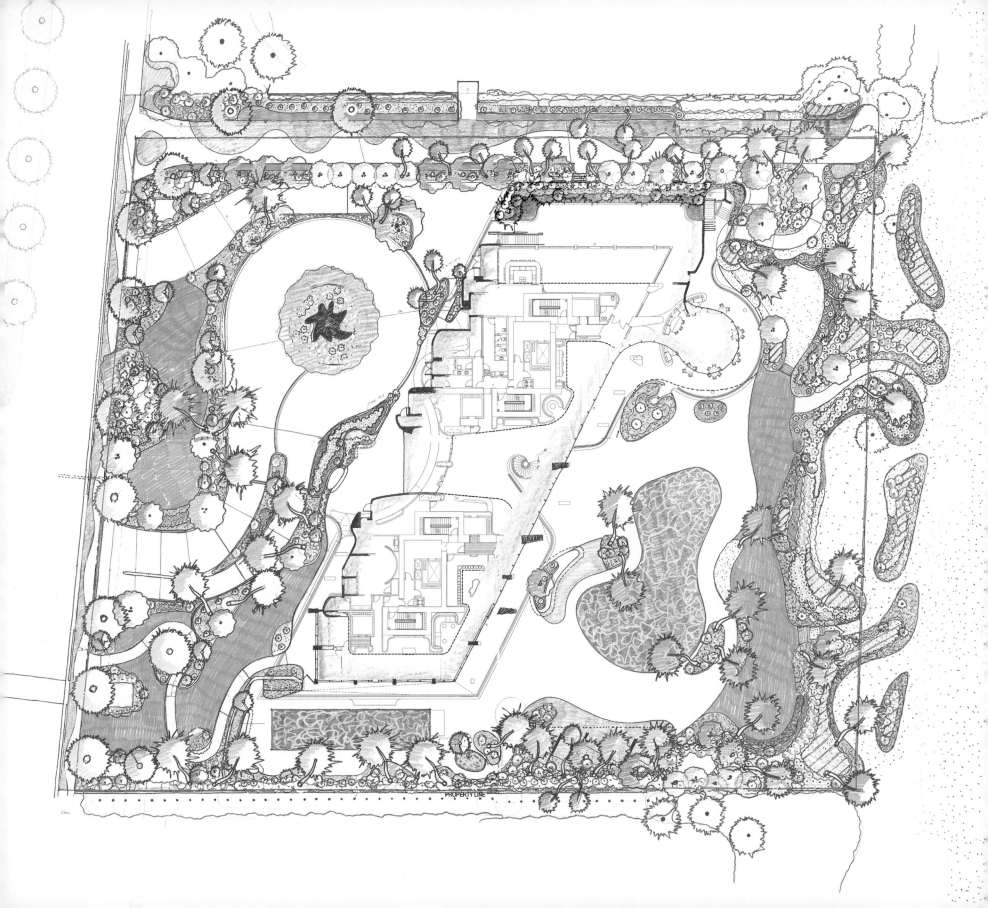

PROPERTY LINE

PRECEDING PAGES: The oceanfront Amenity Garden features a curvilinear pool and terrace as well as more secluded seating on the projecting balcony.

OPPOSITE AND ABOVE: Herzog & de Meuron's decision to design a parallelogram footprint minimizes the skyscraper's shadow on the beach and maximizes the amount of direct sun that the ocean-facing apartments receive. This gesture, along with underground parking, gave Jungles room to design exceptional garden spaces.

OVERLEAF: Residents walk along the sand path to access the ocean. The dune has been restored with resilient plant material including *Conocarpus erectus* var. *sericeus*, *Heliotropium gnaphalodes L.*, *Chrysobalanus icaco* 'Horizontal', *Eragrostis elliottii*, *Gaillardia pulchella*, *Suriana maritima*, and *Hymenocallis latifolia*.

ABOVE: Jungles designed secluded pocket beaches beneath existing *Cocos nucifera* for extended days spent on the sand and in dappled shade.

RIGHT: The organic shape of the pool complements the ribbon element of the architecture. Salt tolerant *Thrinax radiata* palms grow beneath *Cocos nucifera*.

LEFT: *Ernodea littoralis*, commonly known as golden creeper, reaches down through the lobby level architectural ribbon.

OPPOSITE: Boomerang-shaped white stucco planter benches complement the undulating shape of the pool coping.

JADE SIGNATURE GARDEN 115

MASÍA EOLO

With a passion for the wilderness, the clients love to hike the trails within the Panamanian mountains, and they enjoy a slow-paced, close-knit community lifestyle that starkly contrasts with life in nearby Panama City. In search of a weekend retreat, the couple purchased 3.7 acres in the mountains from close friends who share their love of nature, plants, and gardens.

An open expanse of land once used as a chicken farm, the site lies within an ancient volcanic crater, adjacent to an indigenous community and steep forested slopes at the rim, where native plants are preserved in their primeval conditions.

On the initial visit, the architect was discouraged by the featureless land, but Jungles was inspired by the distant views of the unspoiled verdant landscape and geologic character of the ancient volcano rim. Critical viewsheds he highlighted guided the development of the site and grading plans. The project was done in phases. First, the entire site was graded, and the platforms for future residences were created. Next, the gardens were implemented, with Jungles participating in all grading, boulder placement, and plant layout.

The overriding concept was to restore the flat site to a more naturally appearing landform, thus melding the garden with the adjacent forest. To generate fill to build an undulating topography, a central lake was excavated. With an annual rainfall of more than 70 inches, the lake is also a point to harvest on-site and off-site rainwater. The uphill slope was used to aerate the site water through a series of pools, and boulder-filled cascades. The lake enriches the habitat and biodiversity of the area and magnifies the beauty of its context through its reflective nature.

Jungles worked with the clients in identifying flowering trees in the forest to install on the property so that the garden would be a continuation of the forest and habitat. Plant material was purchased from local nurseries, collecting a wide variety of plants to establish native species richness throughout the site. The clients also brought in trees from local nurseries. Much of the landscape plan was put into the ground before the buildings were completed. The clients led the installation of the adjacent gardens based on the conceptual planting plan and improvising where appropriate, a tribute to their knowledge and enthusiasm for the process.

Guests at Masía Eolo now enjoy the show of migrating bird flocks across a site that was once filled with caged chickens. The nocturnal sound of nature rejoicing across the newly regenerated land provides a wild backdrop for the stories created among good friends and family. Jungles himself returns to visit. While photographer Steve Dunn was on-site capturing the garden, he and the clients hiked up and along the crater rim and experienced the wild side of Panama with trails through unspoiled forest and alpine plantings.

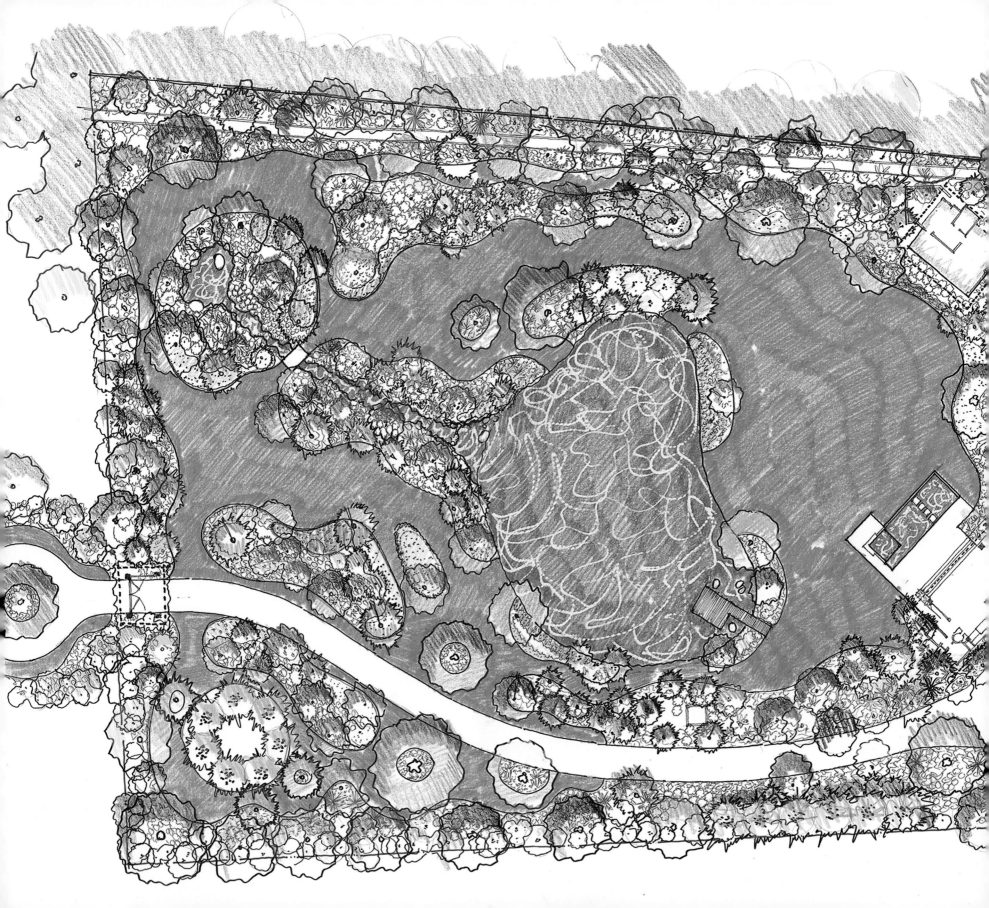

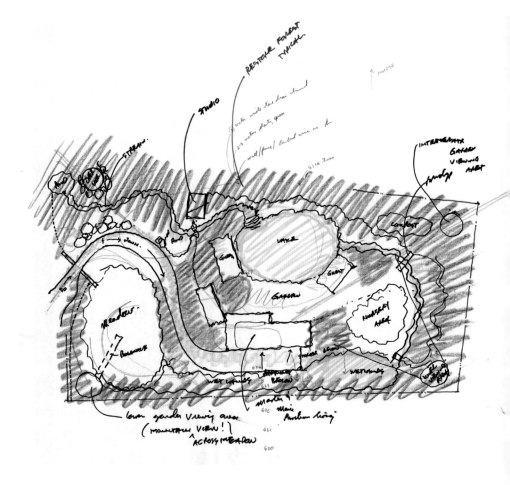

PRECEDING PAGES: The new lake has transformative power. Lawn swaths act as a safety measure for the occasional snake that manages to get through the site's well-concealed perimeter fence.

ABOVE: An early concept sketch shows the intent to harvest and direct rainwater to ponds and wetlands to create wildlife habitat. Topography was a major consideration in the design process.

LEFT: The entire planting design was laid out on site based mostly on locally sourced plant material.

OVERLEAF: View across the lake toward the residence. Great care was taken to screen out future home sites.

OPPOSITE: Trees with high canopies from the forest were introduced to meld the garden and forest, as were native palms.

ABOVE: The waterfall descends from the highest section of the property. The cascade was created with boulders excavated during the grading process. The water provides movement and sound in the garden.

The residence is aligned with the most dramatic distant view—the rupture of the volcano's crater rim, the point where most of the lava flowed.

ABOVE: The entry elements were designed by the developer in a vernacular, country style. Jungles designed the concrete vine trellis, inspired by a local detail seen in the community.

OPPOSITE: Grandchildren and adults enjoy fishing and launching boats from the dock, which is supported by boulders placed over the pond liner.

OVERLEAF: Plant details, from upper left: *Vriesea* 'Mint Julep', *Pinanga kuhlii*, *Chambeyronia macrocarpa*, *Colocasia esculenta* 'Black Magic', and *Calliandra surinamensis*.

EL ALEAR GARDEN

Located within the community of Antigua Hacienda de Carrizalejo, El Alear is south of the city of Monterrey with the Sierra Madre Oriental Mountains as a dramatic backdrop. Once a rural community, the area is now incorporated into the city and has been developed with multi-family compounds that offer both security and an array of amenities to residents.

With access from Ave. Roberto Garza Sada, a primary and busy thoroughfare, multiple entry portals give residents and guests the ability to quickly and safely move out of the heavy traffic and enter various subterranean garages or arrive at the landscaped gardens at the entry to the four residential towers. Jungles worked with the architectural team to create a meandering arrival experience with informal planters formed from locally sourced stone. Retaining walls, stairs, and ramps along the drive mitigate the elevation change between the main road and the building entries. Individual porte-cochères are strategically placed and integrated within and around the landscape to soften the architectural lines and provide protection from the elements.

To the south of the residential towers are the major amenity areas for the residents. These are stacked on three levels that help to navigate and fully utilize the grade change across the southern half of the site. The upper amenity area contains the lounge pool, spa, and entertainment deck accommodating sunbathing, large gatherings, and programmed activities.

Emerging from the center of the upper terrace is the sunken paddleball court and fitness center, a program requirement that could have seized a large amount of landscape area. Jungles worked with the architect and developer for an alternative solution. Ultimately a portion of the subterranean garage was allocated for this use, concealing the function, but still maintaining garden views from the recreational facility. This fitness area is covered by a green roof, which provides a desirable view from the apartments above and allows stormwater collection.

A grand set of garden stairs running adjacent to the fitness center allows one to proceed from the upper garden level to the mid-level terrace with the lap pool and additional gathering areas for dining or entertaining. Positioned along the linear edge of the lap pool is the second set of stairs and a ramp

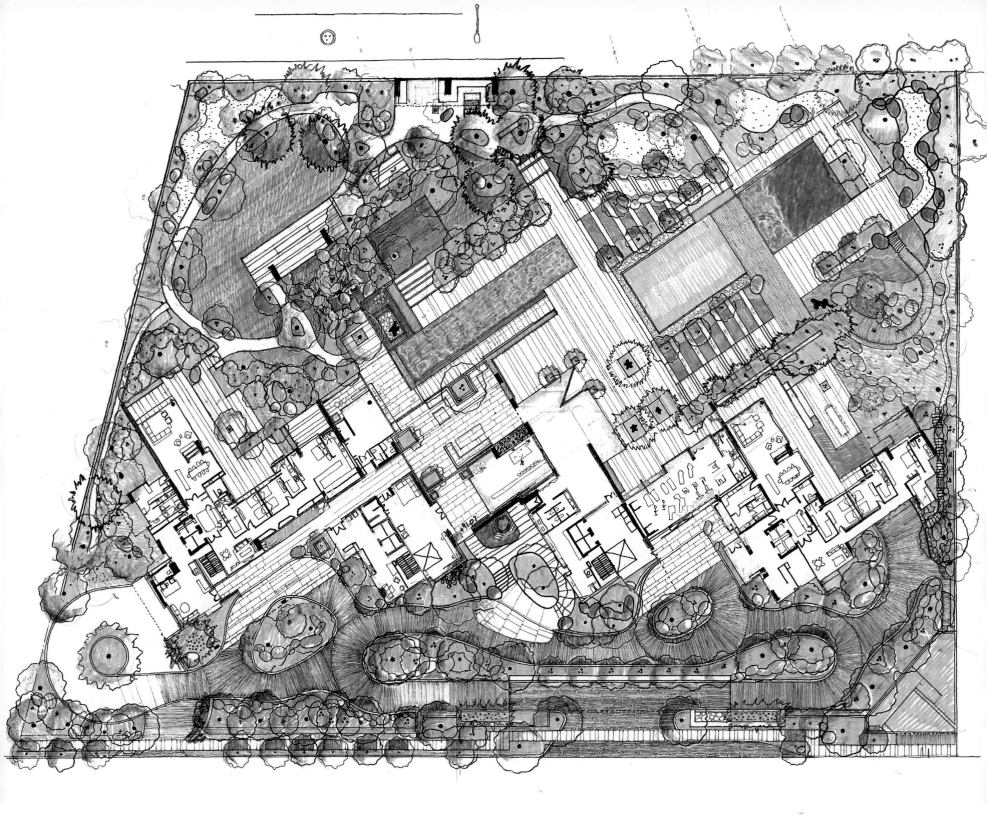

OPPOSITE: The site plan shows the stone walls that flow through the property, allowing the circulation paths, driveways, and gardens to traverse the topographical challenges of the site. The rough and organic nature of the walls is a nod to the construction methods of the region and contrast to the refined architectural style.

RIGHT: Residents and guests are greeted by planters that soften the facade of the residential towers. Shade structures with carefully integrated trees provide a comfortable arrival and departure experience.

that is integrated into the wall of the pool, becoming an elegant water feature along the procession and generating ambient noise for the garden.

The far southeast corner of the garden is dedicated to more passive uses. A gradually sloping lawn was created for families, children, and pets to play as they please. An "arroyo" or dry stream basin that collects runoff during major storm events is integrated into the landscape with natural boulders found on site. Several nature trails traverse the 3.3 acres of gardens and outdoor areas offering opportunities for residents to commune with the outdoors in a passive setting.

All the garden and activity areas face the mountain ranges, creating vignettes and interest throughout the site. The planting itself is composed entirely of native species that evoke the characteristics of the nearby Chipinque Ecological Park. While the need for irrigation is reduced by utilizing drought-tolerant plant material, minimal irrigation is provided by two large cisterns that collect stormwater run-off and air-conditioning condensate from the buildings. Along with the irrigation system, infrastructural systems are hidden throughout the garden spaces, including CCTV, audio equipment, telecommunications and data. These discreet systems allow for increased security and provide a sense of comfort for the residents.

LEFT: Water from the fitness pool cascades to the garden below. Trail systems lead away from the residential cluster providing additional opportunities for passive recreation.

OPPOSITE: The fitness center is covered in green, enhancing the view from the apartments above.

OPPOSITE: The subtle cascading water wall from the fitness pool shimmers in the evening light.

RIGHT: A gradual stair leads residents to the upper level and a dramatic view out to the surrounding mountain range.

RIGHT BELOW: The lounge pool and surrounding decks offer ample entertaining spaces within gardens that afford privacy from neighbors.

OVERLEAF: Vegetation is strategically placed to screen the surrounding residences and create privacy. A green roof covers the paddleball court and fitness center; expansive glazing allows views out into the garden.

ATRIUM GARDEN
FORD FOUNDATION CENTER FOR SOCIAL JUSTICE

New York, New York | 2019

The restoration of the iconic Atrium Garden at the Ford Foundation Center for Social Justice was part of a full-building reconfiguration of the headquarters designed by Kevin Roche of Kevin Roche John Dinkeloo Associates and completed in 1967. Both the building and the garden are designated New York City landmarks.

The Atrium Garden, originally designed by the Office of Dan Kiley, was imagined and installed as a temperate New England forest. Kiley's plant selections included more than 40 trees, 1,000 shrubs, and 22,000 vines and groundcover. His tree selections allotted open sightlines from 42nd to 43rd Street for light penetration while also complementing the atrium's monumental scale and creating an intimate garden experience. To navigate the 13-foot change in grade, the design provided pathways at three levels and stairways which served as a throughway.

Kiley used the plants' bloom sequences to mimic nature and seasonality. The understory provided color, fragrance, and texture. The main tree species, *Magnolia, Eucalyptus,* and *Cryptomeria*, were chosen for their presence and form. *Jacaranda* and *Pyrus* were used to enhance the space through color and texture. Ferns and grasses were used to create patterns like dappled light on a forest floor.

Unfortunately, the challenges in the atrium—light requirements, extreme slopes, temperature, and humidity constraints—compromised the landscape over time. At the outset of the restoration in 2015, the space looked ad hoc and overly dense, with no direct sightlines. Jungles performed an extensive analysis of the original plan, comparing plants that could survive in the harsh environment. The team was adamant about following Kiley's lead and planting directly into the soil. Driven by deliberate relationships, the planting strategy was executed so that the garden would grow stronger with time, allow a careful study of the garden's evolution, and combine Kiley's vision with scientific innovation.

Creating a new ecosystem to support the original design required several innovative approaches. The team made several key adaptations: installing new grow lights, pre-purchasing plants, and acclimating the trees. Fitting the new grow lights presented an initial challenge due to the historic nature of the building. Collaboration with the MEP engineer and architect allowed the team to anticipate the atrium conditions and work to acclimate the trees accordingly. The acclimation period trained trees to thrive in low light conditions. The trees were purchased, root pruned for hardening, then bare-rooted

PRECEDING PAGES: To accommodate a dramatic grade change, the garden was divided into terraces connected by a large staircase and a series of smaller ones.

OPPOSITE: Restoration plan for the atrium floor and for the terrace above. Many view this oasis as a botanical garden in the heart of Midtown Manhattan.

ABOVE: Aerial view of the tree canopy of *Ficus binnendijkii* 'Amstel King', *Calliandra haematocephala*, *Bucida buceras* 'Shady Lady', and *Podocarpus gracilior*. Trees were brought in from 42nd Street through the window wall onto a specially built platform over the fountain. There they were unwrapped, measured, and inspected for damage and pests before being picked up and placed by crane.

and transplanted into custom-fitted boxes. The grade change and resulting steep slopes between paths required technical intervention for tree planting. The eight-month acclimation period had to take the slope into account. The team used the Missouri Gravel Method to create more fibrous root growth and aid the trees' adjustment. The exact slope of the gravel in the box reflected the tree's final location. The trees remained in their boxes and under shade for the duration of the process.

Limited availability of appropriate plant material vital in re-envisioning Kiley's design required tagging larger than anticipated trees. Together with the help of a talented landscape contractor, the team devised an installation plan by bringing a crane into the historic space without damaging the original brick paving. The larger trees were installed by crane, moving, and working them around sizable trees and delicate garden paths. The use of geofibers as a soil additive to hold slopes as steep as 1:1 enabled the larger trees to be planted. The understory mimics Kiley's with ferns, blooming shrubs, and groundcovers.

As a result of the team's innovation, adaptability, and close collaboration during both the design and construction phases, the project is a success. The atrium today is again as Dan Kiley envisioned it.

LEFT AND OPPOSITE: Today the garden looks like the New England forest Kiley envisioned. The towering green canopies and the colorful, textured understory garden beckon passerby from the street. From the offices above, the view is vibrant with clear sightlines across the atrium.

OVERLEAF: The color palette is primarily shades of green. 'Amstel King" Fig trees with twisted trunks replace the original southern magnolias in Kiley's design. Both trees have a similar shape, size, and branching. The new growth on the fig is red, which resembles the copper undersides of magnolia leaves.

The pool at the center is the focal point of the design. Widened entrances, a new wheelchair lift, braille signage, and audio descriptions greatly expand access through the entire space.

OPPOSITE: The versatile tiered garden is the setting for receptions, more intimate outdoor meetings, and informal strolls by those in the neighborhood. Collaboration is an important value of the Ford Foundation, and the new atrium design has helped that value flourish.

ABOVE: The diversity of height, color, and texture of the plantings, the effect of dappled light through the canopies, and the sound of water in the pool are an homage to the New England forest.

COCCOLOBA GARDEN

Islamorada, Florida | 2018

The Coccoloba Garden rests on top of an ancient coral reef that is more than 125 million years old. The project site is seven acres in area, 11 percent of which is protected second-growth native forest with a brackish pond where previous owners quarried fossilized limestone as a part of a commercial shrimp farm operation. The rare fossilized limestone, commonly called "keystone," can be found only in Monroe County, Florida.

Given the length of the drive from the historic Overseas Highway to the waterfront residence, Jungles developed an entry sequence with as many habitats, vistas, and garden spaces as possible; he introduced curves and changes in grade to impart a feeling of surprise and discovery.

To offset construction costs, the pond was enlarged, and lowlands were created to harvest as much keystone as possible. Fill from the excavations was used to vary the flat grade, and keystone monoliths were sold to offset the cost of the proposed keystone pool decking, driveway, and terrace paving. More common Miami Dade County oolite limestone monoliths were used to build retaining walls, floating stepping pads, and sculptural elements. Aquatic consultants stocked the pond with indigenous species of fish that would thrive in the tidal fluctuations and the red mangrove forest environment. Most plant material is from the indigenous Florida Keys landscape, one of the ecosystems with the highest plant biodiversity in the continental United States.

The buildable part of the site is in a flood zone, subject to hurricane storm surges, battering wind, and airborne salt spray. Regulations required raising the building six feet above existing site elevations. Working with the architects Bruce Carlson and Steve Siskind, Jungles endeavored to create a sustainable, naturalistic landscape or landform that would meet code, rising gradually to the required height for the residence.

It was critical to create a garden that could survive the seasonal dry period (approximately half the year), saltwater inundations from storms, and the constant wind bearing airborne salt. With that said, the garden was put to the test upon completion in 2017 when Hurricane Irma made a direct hit. Although there were storm surge related erosion issues and toppled trees, the garden was completely restored within a year's time.

This project reflects the success of great teamwork. Jungles enjoyed collaborating with enlightened clients, talented architects at the helm, great craftsmen and builders, and a knowledgeable landscape contractor with whom he has worked for more than twenty-five years.

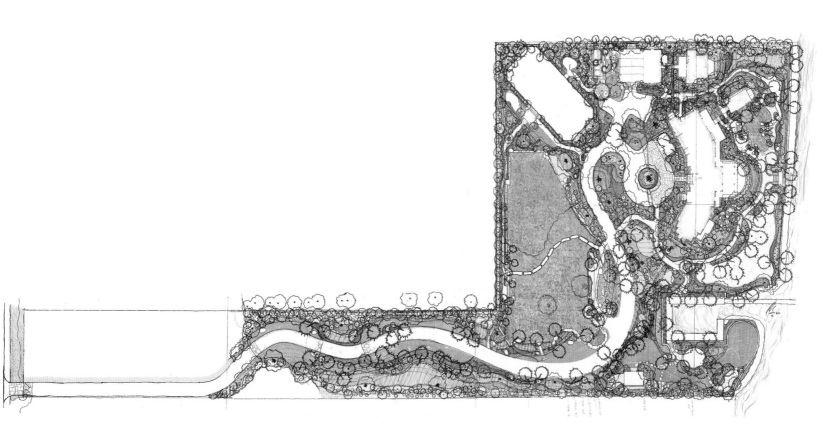

PRECEDING PAGES: A large oolite monolith was carved into a water trough while others were carved into planters with *Alluaudia procera*. Purple flowers from swaths of *Salvia leucantha* and grasses like *Spartina bakeri* and *Solidago sempervirens* thrive in the sandy soils.

ABOVE: Jungles aspired to create as many habitats, vistas, and garden spaces as possible to enliven the drive from the historic Overseas Highway to the waterfront residence.

LEFT: The entry garden is elevated and animated by a curving crushed-shell driveway. The existing hammock was enhanced with understory shrubs and a grove of *Copernicia baileyana* palms.

RIGHT: A specimen *Conocarpus erectus* was relocated to this prominent location where its beauty is now celebrated.

OVERLEAF: An oolite pathway appears to float above the surface of the water. Branches of specimen *Rhizophora mangle* convey a sculptural quality.

OPPOSITE: The pond is filled with fish that thrive in brackish and tidal waters. Beyond is a palapa bar with the Atlantic Ocean in the distance.

ABOVE: Native, salt tolerant plantings like *Baccharis dioica* add texture and drama around a specimen latania palm.

ABOVE: The veranda, accented by a Florida keystone border wall, overlooks the beachfront pool garden.

OPPOSITE: An open-air bridge leads to the summer kitchen. Beneath it, fused stonework and native plantings accentuate the pathway.

This covered bridge links the main house to the guest wing. *Ernodea littoralis* drips down from the oolite monolith walls while native understory trees including *Myrcianthes fragrans* and shrubs including *Capparis cynophallophora* soften the form of the architecture.

The pool was designed to feel like a remnant of a reef exposed
when the sea receded. Jungles worked with Dave Duensing on the
naturalistic stonework.

FAENA HOUSE GARDEN

Faena House sits in the Faena District, a four-block stretch of Collins Avenue that features revitalized historic buildings, such as Roy France's Saxony Hotel (1948) and his art deco Versailles Hotel (1941), and a collection of contemporary designs by leading architectural firms. Jungles designed the streetscapes, public right-of-way improvements, and beachfront gardens to tie the distinct architectural styles together.

The design of the gardens at Faena House draws inspiration from the architecture of Foster + Partners and from the history of Florida's natural systems. The design mimics the changing geometries of nature, fused with the clean architectural elements of the built surroundings by using a shared language of modern intervention, from the architecture to the landscape.

Native plantings weave throughout the exterior, drawing on the region's remarkable biodiversity while integrating the visual and lived experience. Focus is drawn to the viewpoints and areas of contemplation within the garden spaces. Movement within the landscape is encouraged, from shifts in the form and height of the reinstated dune system to the subtle transition of shade and light. Texture and color embrace each other, from the soft silver leaves of silver buttonwood trees to the rough red trunks of gumbo limbo trees. Sea grapes and palm trees elongate views to the ocean and shield views to the street.

Water elements unify the landscape and architecture, encouraging exploration. The spacious pool deck and relaxed, lightweight, multiuse site furnishings allow residents and their guests to create their own lounge areas facing the pool or the ocean. The main swimming pool is more traditional in depth and is long enough for morning laps. As the day progresses and shade begins to blanket the sunny areas, the boardwalks and pool area transition into outdoor relaxation spaces. While the various water features cool them during the day, dancing flames from the fire pit create a warm retreat and casual, social setting at night.

A naturalistic beach just east of the pool area is a respite from the more structured garden and an introduction to the natural edge of the beach and dune system. Sand and movable furnishings create flexibility in the use of the spaces tucked into the garden.

The pool garden and pool are intimately integrated with the elegant architecture in form and spirit. Large slabs of coralina stone impart a casual, yet grand surface with strategically placed, relaxed, comfortable, lounging furniture. Ipe sun decks with low, luxurious chaise lounges speak of seaside residential estates. From the highest elevation east of the residential tower, there are filtered views of the horizon line and blue Gulfstream waters beyond.

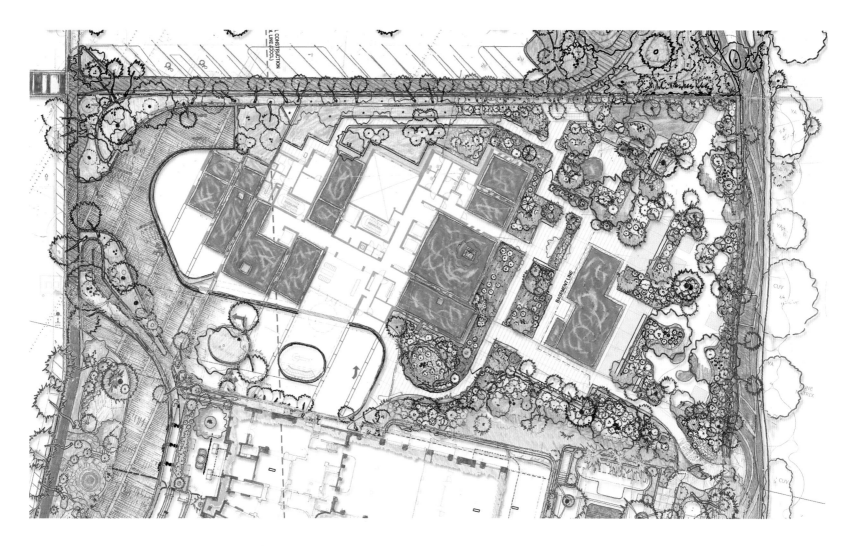

PRECEDING PAGES: Branches of native trees enclose intimate vistas across the pool area and diminish the scale of the adjacent Saxony Hotel. Jungles created a blanket of silvers and greens from silver saw palmetto and sabal palms to green buttonwood and silver buttonwood trees.

The Faena House project (above) is part of the Faena District landscape plan (opposite) developed by Jungles. The Beach Walk is a public promenade that borders the Faena House and Faena Hotel gardens, the natural dune system, and beach. The biomorphic paving pattern incorporates the City of Miami Beach's historic pink pavers.

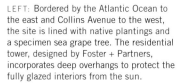

LEFT: Bordered by the Atlantic Ocean to the east and Collins Avenue to the west, the site is lined with native plantings and a specimen sea grape tree. The residential tower, designed by Foster + Partners, incorporates deep overhangs to protect the fully glazed interiors from the sun.

RIGHT: Dominican coralina stone pavers and veneered planters lead the way through the garden to the pool and beach access. Plants include salt-tolerant and wind-tolerant species like *Thrinax radiata* and *Conocarpus erectus* var. *sericeus*.

OVERLEAF: Minimalistic hardscape and lush landscape form an intimate poolside setting. Palms include *Thrinax radiata*, *Sabal domingensis*, and leaning *Sabal palmetto*. A towering *Conocarpus erectus* is adjacent to the spa. The *Plumeria obtusa* will bloom with white fragrant flowers.

Residents can choose between swimming laps or lounging in the shallows while surrounded by a native landscape. Outdoor seating, tucked away amid layers of subtropical plants, creates a wild and luxurious retreat.

LEFT: Access to the beachside entrance of the Faena House is flanked by towering sabal palms.

OPPOSITE ABOVE: Grassy lounge areas are a perfect, wild beach retreat for residents and their guests.

OPPOSITE BELOW: The Beach Walk runs between the property and the beach itself.

179

FIVE PALMS GARDEN

Miami Beach, Florida | 2019

Designed as a single cohesive garden, this project connects three properties to create a family compound along a prominent waterway in Miami Beach. Each of the segments serves a different function. At the center is a large amenity space for friends and family, flanked by the family's inner sanctum to the south and guest quarters to the north. The west-facing infinity edge pools visually extend the presence of water to the waterway beyond. The dark materiality enhances the reflective quality of the water and acts as a window to the sky, mirroring the clouds and fronds of adjacent palm trees.

Jungles joined the project team to conceptualize the planting and hardscape elements, including the pools, water features, seating areas, driveways, planters, and exterior steps. Native Florida keystone was selected for the hard surfaces, while stamped concrete was specified for the driveway. The water features, designed to support koi fish, respected the side yard setbacks for each parcel.

The entire property was elevated by a few feet, allowing the preservation of an existing mango tree between two of the lots. The tree's elongated branching conceals the size of the adjacent residential structure and shades the courtyard space. Shade is an essential element, as the properties face west. Large-scale ipe pergolas visually connect the outdoor spaces and activate the poolside garden for entertaining both day and night.

The individual properties were documented, permitted, and constructed separately due to zoning technicalities. Demolition and construction of the third lot did not begin until the first of the new residences was completed, as the client was occupying the existing structure there. Completion is forthcoming.

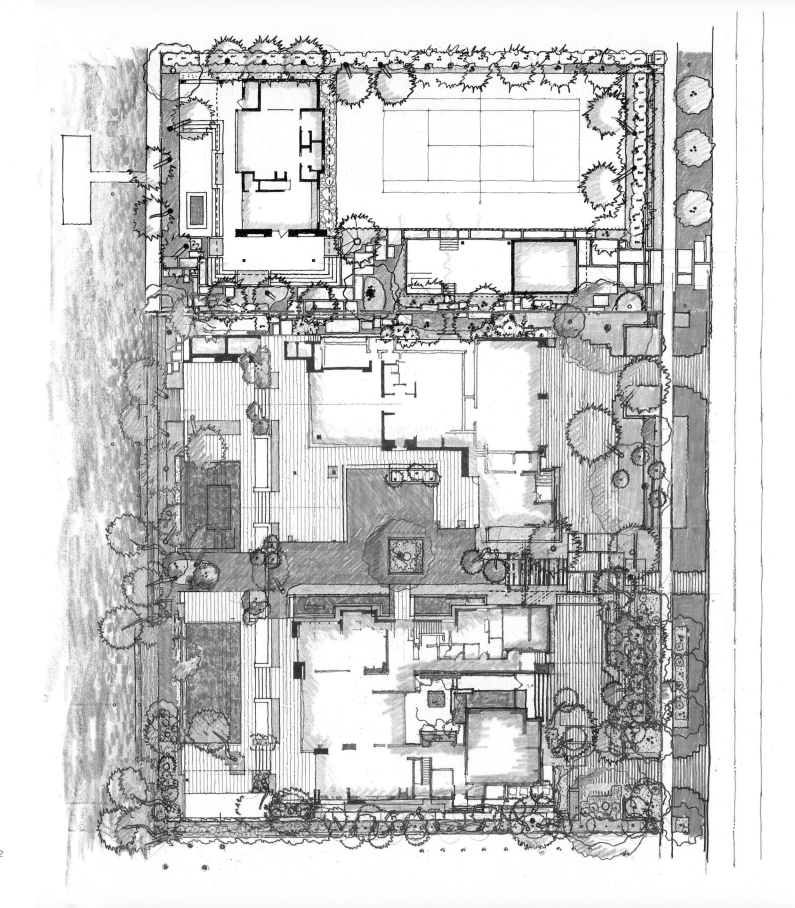

PRECEDING PAGES AND ABOVE: Water features are incorporated into the house at strategic moments. A specimen *Caesalpinia granadillo* tree greets guests as they enter. Jungles detailed the wood bench and koi ponds.

OPPOSITE: The property encompasses three waterfront lots, connected as one through a shared language of landscape and hardscape elements.

The clients requested multiple outdoor garden rooms for entertaining. Jungles designed the trellis structures, which are softened with climbing purple bougainvillea.

The hardscape materiality is seamless throughout. Florida keystone built-in seating, steps, pool deck, and coping add texture and depth to the infinity edge pools.

LEON LEVY NATIVE PLANT PRESERVE

Eleuthera, The Bahamas | 2013

The Leon Levy Native Plant Preserve was conceived in a culture of cooperation, collaboration, and enthusiasm. The Preserve is the fulfillment of the vision of longtime residents Leon Levy and Shelby White, who loved the natural environment and way of life on Eleuthera. After Leon Levy's passing in 2003, Shelby White wanted to celebrate her husband's devotion to the island while contributing to a better future for all Eleutherans.

This 30-acre preserve was jointly created by the Bahamas National Trust and the Leon Levy Foundation. These two organizations have now formed the first national park on Eleuthera, a designated research center for traditional bush medicine, a facility for the propagation of indigenous plants and trees, and an educational center focusing on the importance of native vegetation to the biodiversity of the Bahamas.

The project's primary goal was to raise awareness of Bahamian plant diversity and bush medicine, aligning with one of the six broad areas for the Leon Levy Foundation's philanthropic legacy: preservation of nature and gardens. The project was completed in two phases, both with similar concepts of expanding educational opportunities into the preserve.

The site is composed mostly of elevated, rocky, dry forest (called coppice), and lower degraded areas that had been cultivated. The native ecology was being impacted by flourishing invasive, exotic trees and rubbish from an illegal, on-site dump.

During Phase I, Jungles orchestrated the design and siting of the main structures, including a visitor center, educational pavilion, back-of-house operations center, and restrooms and laid out vehicular and pedestrian circulation and associated parking. Landscape improvements included extensive coppice restoration and the creation of ecosystem-driven gardens including bush medicine exhibition gardens. Phase I also laid the foundation for the visitor experience throughout the preserve, utilizing existing saltwater marsh with a mature stand of red mangroves, secondary dune, and the native coppice as highlighted ecosystems.

The arrival experience is defined by local limestone border walls, built by local masons, and an overhead pergola. Visitors pass over an ancient dune, down to the lowlands to a parking area, planted to feel as if it were etched out of an existing coppice. The pedestrian procession to the visitor center is mysterious, as the path winds through a seemingly pre-existent coppice.

As visitors pass through the building, from garden to garden, the space is enlivened by a cascade of recirculating water down the face of the ancient dune. The water cascade splashes into a lagoon

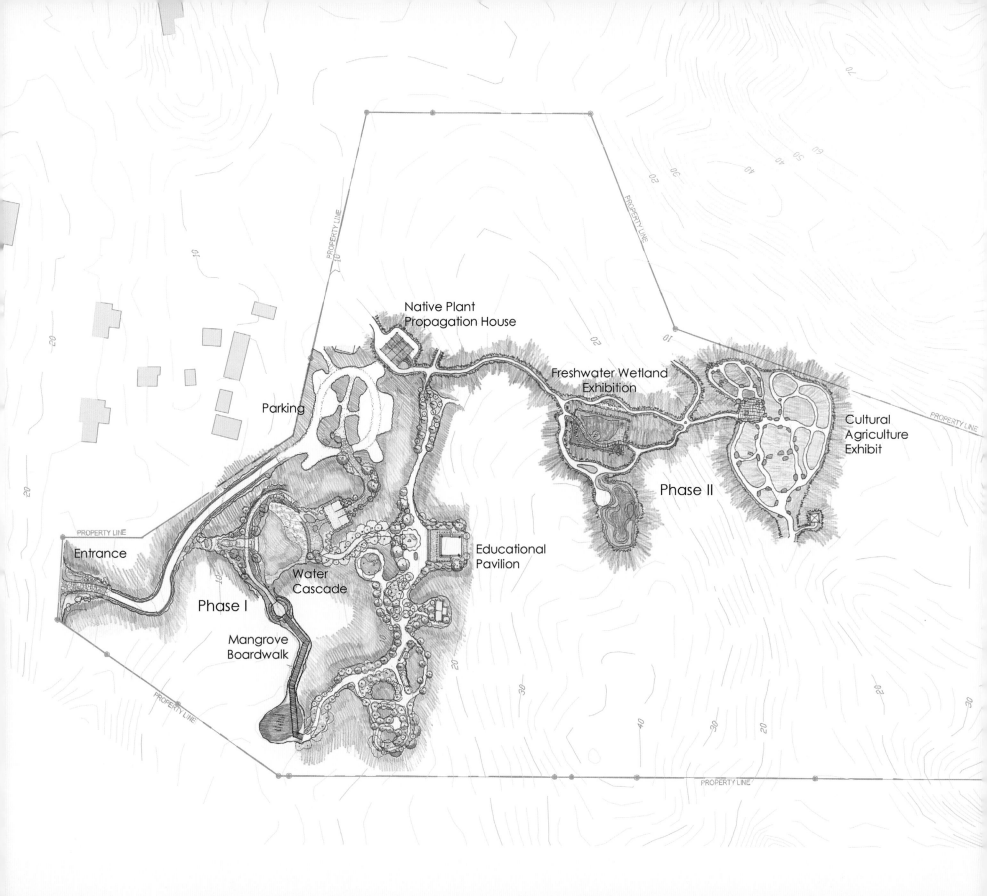

Native Plant
Propagation House

Parking

Freshwater Wetland
Exhibition

Cultural
Agriculture
Exhibit

Phase II

Educational
Pavilion

Entrance

Phase I

Water
Cascade

Mangrove
Boardwalk

PROPERTY LINE

PROPERTY LINE

PROPERTY LINE

PROPERTY LINE

PROPERTY LINE

PRECEDING PAGES: Recycled invasive Australian pine trees have been transformed into towering bird perches in the freshwater wetland exhibition. The Preserve provides important foraging and nesting areas for more than seventy resident and migratory bird species throughout the year.

BELOW: The master plan shows the phased development of the Preserve, incorporating a facility for the propagation of indigenous plants and exhibitions focused on the importance of native vegetation to the biodiversity of the Bahamas.

RIGHT: Jungles's design sketches show the repurposing of a preexisting agricultural cistern into the freshwater wetland exhibition.

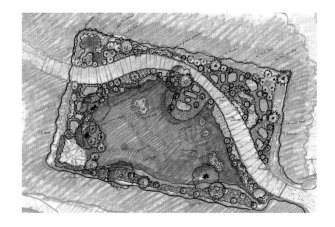

Ethan's Tower

created through the excavation of the dump, below the water table. Soon after its creation, the lagoon was happily inhabited by birds and dragonflies.

After circumnavigating the lagoon and crossing the watercourse, the path descends to a boardwalk that passes through a red mangrove stand. Across the boardwalks are a series of bush medicine exhibitions. The education pavilion, the departure point for nature trails, is a flexible structure that provides shelter for outdoor lessons, weddings, and other group gatherings. All trail systems lead to the visitor center as well as a dramatic viewing tower sited by the Bahamas National Trust botanist Dr. Ethan Freid.

Phase II aspired to feature other Bahamian ecosystems and to expand the educational opportunities available to the Preserve visitors. Major new additions included a native plant propagation center, designed by Jungles, a freshwater wetland created from a pre-existent agricultural cistern, and a historical agricultural exhibition garden. Phase II also incorporated the excavation of underground formations of limestone oxidized through rainwater erosion, exposing hidden site geology to visitors.

By the end of Phase II, 20 percent of the Preserve had been restored to native vegetation and converted into accessible gardens. It has become a sanctuary for humans, animals, and insects. The public has embraced the Preserve, and record numbers of visitors are spreading awareness of this native oasis. Jungles found the project rewarding, collaborating with a variety of stakeholders, including the local community to unearth the best solutions to the project's challenges. He is now designing Phase III, an additional five acres of land, which will include an expanded visitor center, accommodations for students and scientists, faculty lodging, maintenance and administrative facilities, an event pavilion, an event lawn, a water garden, and many new trail systems.

In April 2019, the Leon Levy Native Plant Preserve became the first institution in the Bahamas to be designated an accredited botanic garden by Botanic Gardens Conservation International. This tier of accreditation recognizes institutions for their achievements in plant conservation.

TOP: The excavation of the illegal dump revealed an eroded layer of prehistoric reef. To animate the visitor's experience and to aid in the aeration of the mangrove lagoon, a manmade waterfall was created using local Bahamian limestone.

ABOVE AND RIGHT: A processional pedestrian experience through the restored native woodlands leads into the visitor center, designed as a portal. Jungles calls it a "non-building."

Varying depths of water in the freshwater wetland exhibition provide habitat for a multitude of local flora and fauna including native Bahamian freshwater turtles who enjoy coming to the water's edge to be fed.

The Preserve is designed to be an educational resource for students from kindergarten through high school to explore wildlife and engage in activities that encourage environmental awareness and individual stewardship for the natural world around them.

SWAN GARDEN

Swan is an indoor-outdoor dining destination in the heart of the posh Miami Design District conceived by hospitality mavens David Grutman and Pharrell Williams. What was once a surface parking lot servicing a one-story retail showroom is now an urban oasis of green.

Craig Robins, developer of the Miami Design District, enlisted Grutman and Williams to provide an additional food-and-beverage venue within this creative neighborhood represented by more than one hundred high-end fashion storefronts. The 13,500-square-foot restaurant and second-floor lounge fuses modern cuisine with a premier alfresco ambiance for patrons to see and be seen amid the reverberations of the live DJ sets.

Ken Fulk's interior design genius and Jungles's garden vision work in harmony to create an Instagramable setting, a highlight that the clients are known for worldwide. Jungles worked with Fulk to design all the hardscape elements, though David Grutman ultimately designed the entry water feature.

The site is enveloped by a beautiful garden fence and entry gate woven with vines. On arrival, guests pass beneath the sculptural canopies of two specimen *Clusia rosea* trees. Additional mature *Clusia rosea* and mahogany trees become focal points in various areas of the exterior dining area, augmented by other native understory trees.

The clients wanted something different. Swan has a wilder look, where plants spill out of the space and become the most distinguished features. The garden's success prompted Robins to request permission to repeat our planting palette in other areas of the neighborhood. We gladly accepted.

When dining winds down in the late evening hours, guests migrate to the upstairs lounge that includes an outdoor terrace. We wanted to create inviting circulation from upstairs to downstairs while activating the terrace and providing another egress route for fire codes. This led us to our design of a staircase that essentially disappears into the plantings. The base of the staircase has since become a popular destination for "selfies."

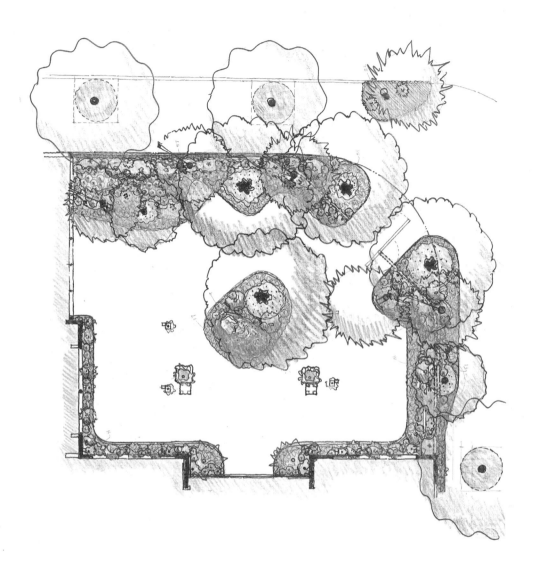

PRECEDING PAGES: Beyond the dense masses of *Clusia rosea* trees, a wood gate swings open, inviting fashionable patrons into Swan, where celebrities, pro-athletes, and foodies gather for extended brunches or dinners that last well past midnight.

ABOVE: Jungles worked with interior designer Ken Fulk to create a courtyard that felt private and interior-facing. This space is the heartbeat of the luxury retail and cultural destination. It also doubles as a refuge, where one can linger for hours and sway to the beat of the DJ.

RIGHT: Textures of green foliage pair nicely with pops of color from flowering orchid plants growing on the branches of *Clusia rosea* trees. *Neomarica caerulea* 'Regina', *Philodendron* 'Weeks Red Hybrid', and *Musa balbisiana* 'Black Thai' add depth.

OPPOSITE: The staircase leads to an outdoor deck that connects to Bar Bevy, the upstairs lounge. Pink permeates the interior bar and seating areas, while many shades of green add a wildness to the outdoor dining experience.

ABOVE: Light streams through the slats of the recycled greenheart wood pivot gate engulfed in *Monstera deliciosa*.

MIAMI BEACH BOTANICAL GARDEN

Miami Beach, Florida | 2011, 2020

Miami Beach Botanical Garden, created in 1962 as a city park, is a 2.6-acre green space in the heart of the city that makes up in tremendous diversity of plant life what it lacks in size. In 2007 Jungles developed a landscape renovation plan, working with the public-private partnership of the Miami Beach Garden Conservancy and the City of Miami Beach. Within the constraints of a somewhat limited budget, Jungles and his team decided to make the most of what was already there, changing elements that would have the most impact and creating a variety of garden rooms. The design is ultimately about an articulation of spaces: gathering spaces, spaces for contemplation, intimate spaces, and public spaces.

A new, processional entry unfolds gradually as visitors move into the garden spaces. Jungles created a very long sight line from the main gate, which seems to magnify the scale of the elements that are immediately visible. A new water garden at the center of the space welcomes the sky into the garden, animates the space, and enlivens the landscape. On a practical level, water also aids in cooling the areas directly around the buildings.

The garden is a regular stop for migratory birds such as warblers, American redstarts, and finches. Permanent residents include an array of cardinals, herons, hawks, and egrets. Butterflies and moths happily feed off the native host nectar plants. Turtles reside in the ponds, along with koi and cichlid fish. A new apiary fosters the growing honeybee population.

Native plants, once only tucked into a designated corner of the garden and treated as a novelty, are now distributed throughout, and their performance in the urban environment is highlighted. Large quantities of these are layered to weave together the urban habitat; they also attract and provide refuge for insects, birds, and other creatures, which in turn enrich and enliven the space. The garden's horticulturalist gave Jungles a "wish list" of plants to incorporate into his design; Jungles added as many as possible, and the final plant palette includes flowering trees, palms, cycads, and other subtropical plants.

Jungles and his team also suggested relocating the nursery and propagation areas to the northeast corner of the garden to improve circulation through the public spaces. This intervention allows the garden to schedule simultaneous events on the grand lawn and exterior terraces, increasing visitation and generating additional rental revenue. Social gatherings include the garden's annual outdoor "Taste of the Garden," a weekly green market, garden yoga, theatrical performances, and private wedding receptions.

The Collins Canal Promenade was completed in summer 2020 during the garden's sudden closure due to the pandemic. The meandering walkway flows into the garden from the northern perimeter. It is augmented by a shaded canopy of palms, native shrubs, and flowering groundcovers.

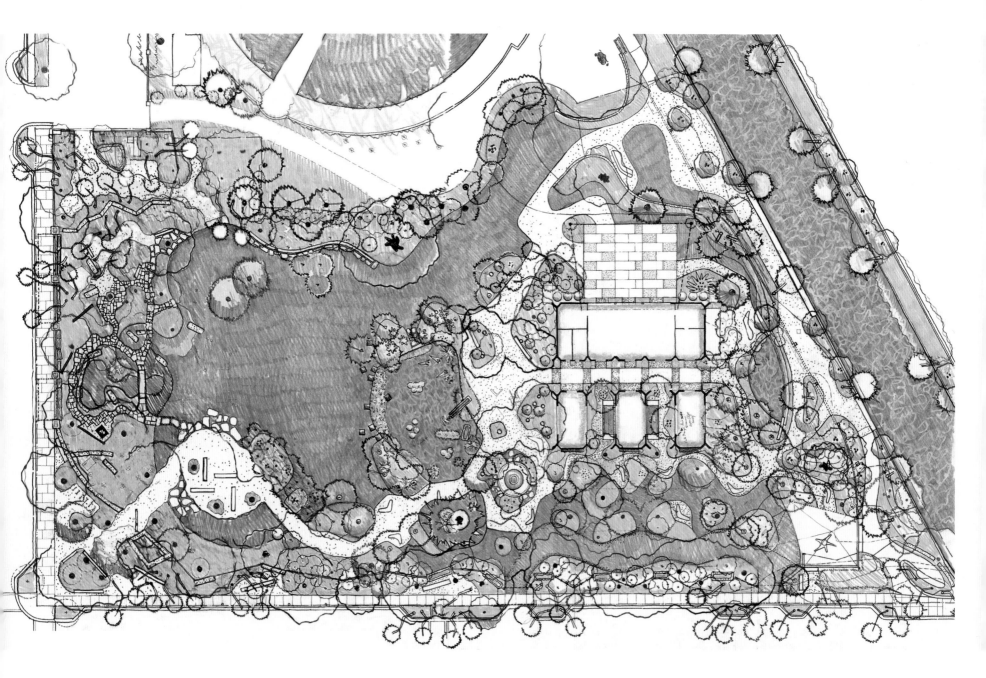

PRECEDING PAGES: The canopy of an existing silk floss tree shelters the main entrance to the garden. Jungles dedicated a large portion of the property, outside of the entry gates, as a shaded public plaza.

ABOVE: The diminutive botanical garden offers a peaceful respite from the surrounding urban environment. Jungles created a sense of entry where there was none. He brought in elements of water to reflect the sky, improved circulation, and linked native plants throughout.

OPPOSITE: A concrete pathway, with a rock-salt finish, weaves through the space.

LEFT: A monolith of oolite stone was carved into a fountain. It floats over the pond and gently spills water into it, creating movement and sound.

RIGHT: The garden is activated daily, with plant tours, art exhibits, food festivals, dance classes, yoga classes, and concerts. Jungles donated the *Corypha umbraculifera* as a 25-gallon plant. It is truly spectacular!

LEFT: A grove of *Libidibia ferrea* trees provides shade above sculptural concrete benches.

RIGHT: A rich textural mix of *Copernicia macroglossa*, an iconic curving *Sabal palmetto*, and *Beaucarnea recurvata*.

FAR RIGHT: Wildflowers and grasses envelop the water garden.

1111 LINCOLN ROAD

Described as an "urban glade," Jungles's redesign for the historic promenade and plaza at 1111 Lincoln Road, developed concurrently with Herzog & de Meuron's now-iconic parking garage, creates a civic space unlike any other in the city. Native plants and hardscape elements are carefully placed to create vantage points and visual corridors for pedestrians—one of the principal goals of the project. Sight lines through the block are also preserved, thanks to massings of low plants and high tree canopies, to ensure that visitors can engage with retail, residential, and restaurant spaces along both sides of the street.

To bring nature into the center of Miami Beach along this roadway-turned-greenway, Jungles looked to the Everglades—a region with unique characteristics and a wide variety of indigenous plants—for inspiration. An ensemble of trees native to Florida and geometric water gardens reminiscent of the famous wetland ecosystem create an inviting gathering space, and turtles, birds, fish, and the sounds of gently cascading water enliven the setting. The highly reflective pond surfaces also mirror the sky, trees, and visitors, adding extra dimension to the narrow urban site.

Specimen cypress trees anchor the display of vegetation within the plaza; other indigenous trees also feature prominently in the design, including live oaks, pond apples, red mangroves, and sabal palms. One nonnative tropical wetland tree was included as well—a Guiana chestnut tree. This "money tree" is indigenous to Central and South American countries. Besides tolerating shade and high-water tables, it is a symbol of good fortune. It was selected for all these qualities and placed where other trees might falter.

The pond maintenance equipment and mechanical systems for the 1100 block are contained in a sculptural vault that is melded into the design of the plaza through a series of stepped platforms. These reduce the impact of its scale, which is further concealed by plants that cascade and a water element that flows slowly between the bold roots of the red mangroves. Climbing to the top has become an attraction for adventurous children and adults, and each stage of the ascent provides a different vantage point.

The materiality of Brazilian *pedra portuguesa* led to its use on the ground plane and throughout the hardscape features. Its mosaic-like texture adds a handcrafted quality to the space and has the additional benefit of gently discouraging skateboarders. Each stone was laid by hand in the style of Roberto Burle Marx. Generously proportioned concrete benches accommodate daily visitors as comfortably as small crowds viewing performances in the space.

PRECEDING PAGES: The plantings for 1111 Lincoln Road are inspired by the Everglades. Silva Cell technology enabled the use of mature cypress and oak trees, brought in to provide immediate shade and scale. White and black *pedra portuguesa* pavement was used to create a pattern reminiscent of the public spaces in Brazil.

ABOVE: Accentuated by the linear site condition, the planting palette, hardscape, and water elements engage pedestrians and establish an "urban glade." Site challenges included the proximity of the high water table and differences in light penetration due to the varied height of the adjacent buildings.

OPPOSITE: The sculptural vault, which conceals the mechanical equipment for all four of the water features, transforms into a stage for a yoga instructor during this impromptu class set between leaning *Sabal palmetto* and multi-trunk *Quercus virginiana*.

The overhangs of the buildings and the canopies of the trees create a comfortable, shaded environment. Although restaurants line the block, outdoor seating is restricted to preserve the plaza space for pedestrians. The roots of a *Rhizophora mangle* anchor the plant into the water, as they would in its natural environment.

Plants and people flourish in this public plaza—a garden that elevates the importance of flora and fauna. *Crinum americanum* blooms in the easternmost water garden at the base of a mighty cypress tree. The wetland plantings are part of the site's extensive biofiltration system.

SKY GARDEN

This garden is the crown on the now-iconic parking garage designed by Herzog & de Meuron for the western end of Lincoln Road. The structure has been recognized around the world for its bold and unexpected architecture, and it has quickly become one of the most visible and recognizable structures in the city.

This project, known as the Sky Garden, gave Jungles the opportunity to enhance a unique rooftop space complementing a penthouse on the top level of the complex, which is otherwise part parking garage, part retail space, and part event space. The overall goal was to strike a balance between aesthetic vision and practicality. Although its high position provides an enviable view of the city and its prominent address gives it instant distinction, the residence is meant to be unpretentious and to defer to the rooftop landscape for its true sense of identity.

The west side is called the Slope Garden, acknowledging the way the slanted approach to the penthouse angles down gradually underneath the westernmost edge of the garage roof; it eventually levels off ten feet below. The Slope Garden provides an ideal vantage point for views across Biscayne Bay and toward the downtown Miami skyline. The garden was, of necessity, designed to be resilient and low maintenance. A diverse palette of native plants and non-invasive specimen plant material has adapted well to the site and to the shallow soil depths, which average six inches. Specimen red-trunk acacia trees from Africa provide scale and sculptural qualities while framing views toward the Atlantic Ocean in the distance. A winding *Zoysia* grass path—left unmown to celebrate its natural mounding tendency—leads visitors through a variety of experiential moments within the space. Vines, including railroad vine, Virginia creeper, and grape, climb up and over the roof of the garage and the private elevator tower above it and hang suspended over the perimeter railings, giving parking patrons below a clue about the garden's existence.

The east side of the garden, dubbed the Entertainment Garden. rests on the roof of the adjacent building—the former SunTrust bank, originally constructed in 1968. It includes a bar, an outdoor dining table designed by the architects, and a pool designed by Jungles. Open hardscape areas accommodate large gatherings. The area that once housed mechanical equipment has become a spectacular pool framed by leaning sabal palms, a verdant vine trellis, and an outdoor dining area— an extreme example of adaptive reuse.

The Sky Garden uses many of the materials found on the public plaza below, known as 1111 Lincoln Road, which was also designed by Jungles. White *pedra portuguesa* stones were hand-laid and mortared on all exterior horizontal surfaces, while white river rock lines organically shaped planting beds. Cast-in-place concrete slabs in the garage function as floor plates, columns, and ramps. Overall, the Sky Garden's cohesive garden and hardscape design help two very different but equally iconic structures communicate well at the roof level.

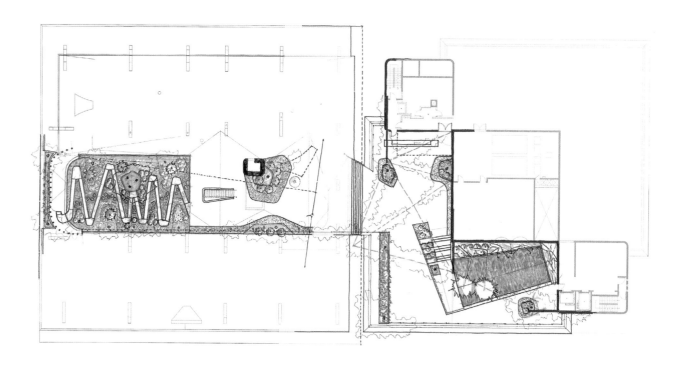

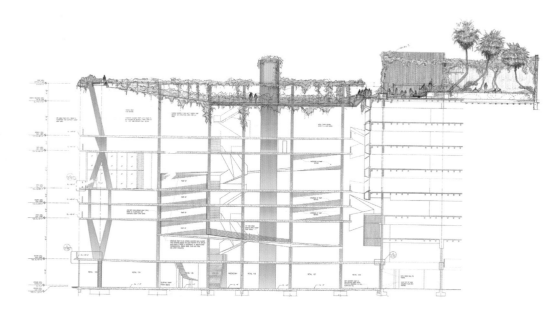

PRECEDING PAGES: The lushly planted rooftop offers panoramic views of the Miami skyline.

ABOVE AND LEFT: The garden extends over the parking garage and fronts the new penthouse designed by Herzog & de Meuron on the adjacent SunTrust building. The pool, planted steps, paving treatment, and green areas were planned in close collaboration with architect Christine Binswanger.

RIGHT: Plants chosen for this extraordinarily sited roof garden thrive in shallow soil and can withstand harsh winds and direct sunlight.

LEFT: The sculptural form of the *Acacia seyal* trees provide drama, shade, and scale. They are complemented by *Alcantarea odorata, Zoysia* spp., and seasonal wildflowers that evoke a natural meadow.

ABOVE AND RIGHT: Tough vines thrive here and often cascade over the seventh floor of the mixed-use garage and retail center. The South Beach skyline is framed by the concrete columns of the structure.

OVERLEAF: Stainless-steel vine cables provide a structure for *Ipomoea pes-caprae*, which becomes living architecture. Plants unite the two contiguous roofs into one plane of green.

CASA BAHIA GARDEN

Coconut Grove, Florida | 2015 and 2019

The Casa Bahia Garden sits on an idyllic waterfront lot in Coconut Grove with sensational water views and a full vista of the downtown Miami skyline. Filmmaker-turned-designer Alejandro Landes worked with Jungles, Zyscovich Architects, and his mother, Catalina Echavarría, to design the "tropical modern" house, which appears to float above the land in homage to the expansive waters of Sailboat Bay.

As a building on the last open waterfront property in the community, the footprint and massing of the structure were scrutinized by a strict homeowners' association, and the clients agreed to many setbacks and unobstructed viewsheds. Jungles conceptualized a minimal hardscape plan focused on loose gravel and a beach-chic plant palette primed for the occasional saltwater inundation from high tides and hurricanes.

When the house went on the market, one of Jungles's clients purchased the property. Jungles worked with the new owner on a modified concrete driveway design, a new alfresco deck for dining by the water, and improved access to the 70-foot-long swimming pool. Now, new walkways traverse the property, and a dock area fosters water sports.

Retaining the strong elements of the existing landscape, Jungles customized the garden to the taste of the new owners, bringing in specimen plants from their neighboring property, including a rare palm collection of *Corypha umbraculifera*, *Copernicia gigas*, *Copernicia fallense*, and *Copernicia baileyana*. He preserved the specimen green buttonwood tree and moved the sea grape trees to the canal side. A flowering *Bombax speciosa* arrived by barge as a gift from the landscape contractor.

From the street, towering clumps of bamboo and native hammock plantings create a sense of privacy and soften the crisp white architecture. The landscape transitions toward the rear of the property to feature lush, low groundcovers and soaring sabal palms that naturally twist to frame the views from the house.

The landscape and architecture appear to blend effortlessly within an open-air atrium that features a two-story water wall and a dramatic, suspended shell-reef limestone staircase that connects the guest pavilion to the main house. The need for privacy and air circulation led to the selection of reclaimed greenheart dock pilings for vertical screening—something very strong yet organic—to tie the two together. The unique texture and color of the wood slats complement the timeless aesthetic of the structures and create moving shadows throughout the day.

229

PRECEDING PAGES: The wraparound balconies and glazed facades take full advantage of the corner waterfront site.

OPPOSITE: Palms line the inland side of the property to screen out neighboring houses.

ABOVE: The site is a rare palm collector's paradise. Simple hardscape gestures beckon all who visit the property to linger outdoors.

LEFT: A grove of *Pritchardia pacifica*, a *Chorisia speciosa* in full bloom, and an *Albizia niopoides* soften the scale of the structure. Low native shrubs were planted to ensure an unobstructed view to the water for all neighbors.

ABOVE: The open-air dining area lies just beyond the shadow of a spectacular green buttonwood tree.

ABOVE: Dappled sunlight dances across the pathway and through the pivot door entryway.

RIGHT: Existing *Coccoloba uvifera* trees were relocated to this focal point adjacent to the suspended shell-reef limestone staircase. The keystone walkway leads to a wooden deck where kayaks are launched with ease.

ABOVE: The path to the house is lined with *Bambusa oldhamii, Microsorum scolopendrium*, and a dramatic *Copernicia gigas*.

OPPOSITE: Sunrise illuminates the pink swaths of *Muhlenbergia capillaris* and water droplets streaming down from the outdoor shower.

GOLDEN ROCK INN GARDEN

The stewards of Golden Rock Inn, artists Helen and Brice Marden, were attracted to this former eighteenth-century sugar plantation on a quiet, 36-square-mile Caribbean island for the abundance of living creatures that share the ground—green vervet monkeys, hummingbirds, tree frogs, sheep, goats, and donkeys. The natural setting is breathtaking; the building is perched 1,000 feet above sea level on the lower side of Mount Nevis, a towering but inactive volcano. Jungles's collaboration with the Mardens created a mountainside retreat for the soul that feels organic and whole.

Volcanic boulders direct the site hydrology, terrace the soil, and catch the ethereal tropical light. Almost indescribably romantic views toward Montserrat and Antigua are framed through sculpted ficus trees. All the elements that define the art of garden creation are in harmony here: light, stone, water, plants, structure, landform, and sky.

The artists' love of lush, wild vegetation prompted Jungles to design with indigenous species as well as colorful subtropical species from around the world. Both artists worked directly with Jungles on different aspects of the garden's design. He and Helen curated the plant selection with an overall aesthetic in mind and favored unusual and exceptional specimen cycads and succulents to make it a reality. Brice collaborated with him and the on-site implementation specialist, Dave Schroeder, to set unearthed boulders. These were arranged in different locations to create inviting destinations where guests could circulate and experience the garden. Boulders too large to move were simply uncovered and allowed to be appreciated for their own monumental scale.

Other boulders, stones, and pebbles unsettled during the process of building roads, parking areas, and terraces for a new restaurant were saved and sorted according to size. These were later arranged to retain steep slopes, build steps, direct water, or to create pockets of microclimates for certain plants. Five large boulders discovered during the excavation of a new wing for the restaurant and initially shoved unceremoniously off to one side hinted, serendipitously, at what was to become the garden's signature element: an area dubbed "The Rocks."

Terraced, placid lily ponds grace a new dining area around The Rocks, and water trickles in a gentle cascade down a historic wall that once directed water to the plantation's original cistern— restored to collect precipitation for use in irrigating the new garden. The water pours from a wall-top rill onto an unearthed, sculpted boulder and then flows lazily into a grotto.

Jungles created meandering pathways to and between the cottages that play with both intimate and grand moments. Runoff from the mountainside was redirected to improve site hydrology—to retention areas blanketed in thick grasses and wide-leafed *Alocasias*. The ravine's slopes needed to be stabilized, so Jungles took the opportunity to enhance them with textured and colorful plantings, which in turn draw attention to the unique property's centuries-old ruins.

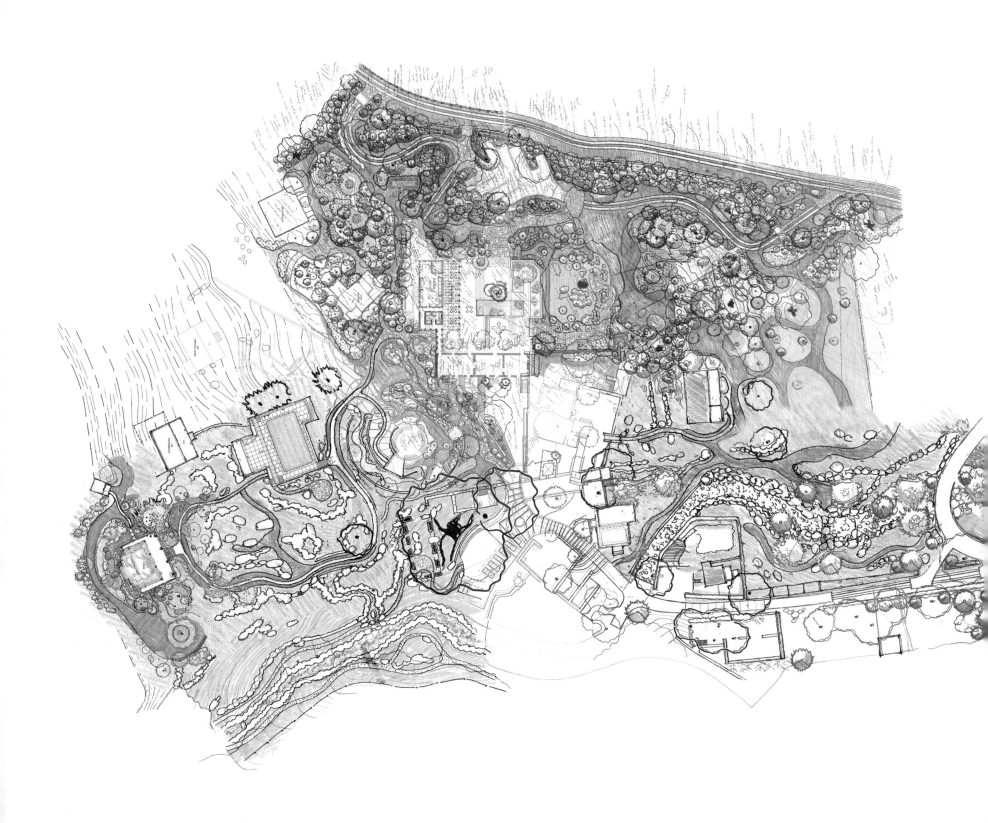

PRECEDING PAGES: Mount Nevis is often masked by heavy cloud cover. The Mardens' love of exotic plants drove the inclusion of *Dioon spinulosum, Dioon mejiae, Spartina bakeri, Aechmea blanchetiana* 'Orange Form', *Attalea cohune, Beaucarnea recurvata,* and *Pachypodium lamerei.* Jungles created an elevated hill that would provide rapid drainage for these plants.

BELOW: Locally available plants and those to be imported to the small island are indicated on this composite planting plan, which was implemented in phases.

RIGHT: An existing *Samanea saman* tree is underplanted with *Aechmea* 'Marcelino', *Kalanchoe gastonis-bonnieri,* and *Philodendron speciosum* to create a tapestry of color and texture.

LEFT: Bold and unusual plants create a visual splendor of green.

ABOVE: The ruins of the historic sugar mill are seen from the uppermost guest cottage. *Dioon edule*, *Encephalartos*, and *Cycas* species are planted above a broad expanse of *Spartina bakeri*.

RIGHT: The buttress-like roots of a *Ceiba pentandra* wrap around remnants of historic sugar plantation structures. The ravine beyond was inundated during the rainy season, so it has been filled and restored with water-loving plants.

OVERLEAF: The island's elusive mountain top appears in a rare moment of clarity. Large-scale plants give the view a dramatic frame, including *Adansonia digitata*, *Aechmea blanchetiana* 'Orange Form', *Coccothrinax miraguama*, *Dioon spinulosum*, *Euphorbia lactea* 'White Ghost', and *Portulacaria afra*.

LILLY BY THE SEA GARDEN

Coconut Grove, Florida

Slated for completion in 2021

OCEAN TERRACE

Miami Beach, Florida

Slated for completion in 2022
Rendering by Elephant Skin

BOSSA HOUSE GARDEN

Marco Island, Florida

Slated for completion in 2022
In conjunction with Studio MK27

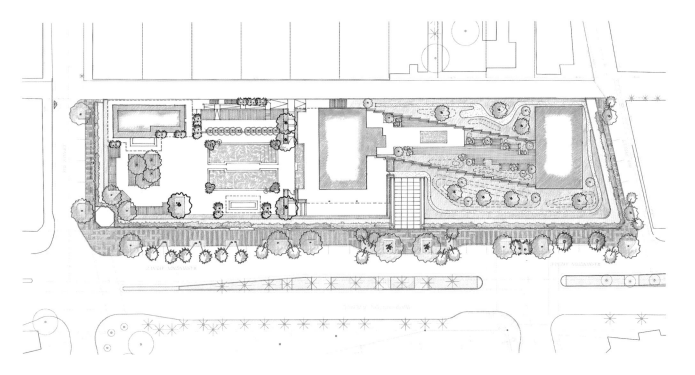

THE GOODTIME HOTEL

Miami Beach, Florida

Slated for completion in 2021
In conjunction with Morris Adjmi Architects,
Ken Fulk, David Grutman, and Pharrell Williams

WORK IN PROGRESS

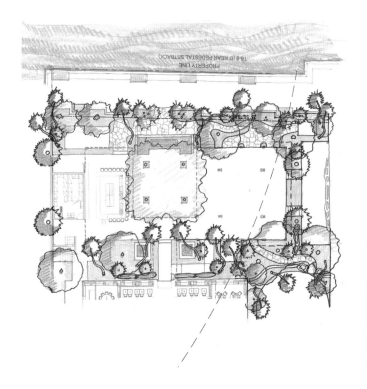

MIAMI WOMEN'S CLUB

Miami, Florida

Slated for completion in 2021
In conjunction with David
Grutman of Groot
Hospitality, TAO Group
Hospitality, Ken Fulk,
and KKAID

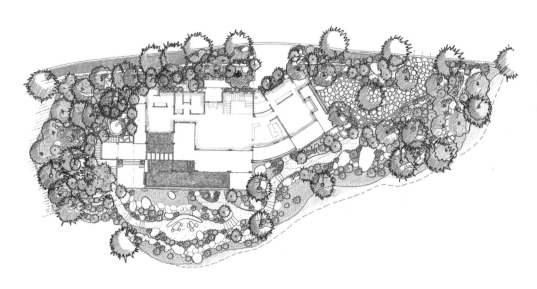

SUNDANCE RIDGE GARDEN

St. Kitts, West Indies

Completed in 2020.

THE COVE

Eleuthera, The Bahamas

Slated for completion in 2021
In conjunction with Gluckman Tang Architects

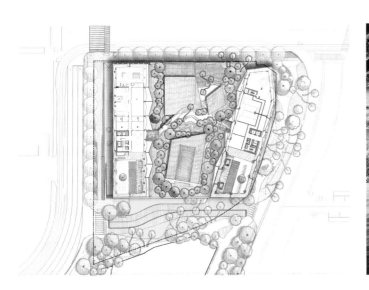

HERON

Tampa, Florida

Slated for completion in 2021
In conjunction with Kohn
Pedersen Fox

WORK IN PROGRESS

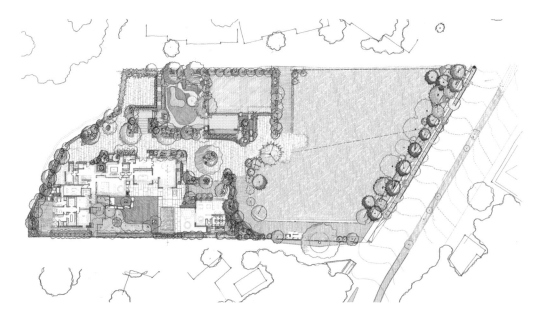

SECRET MOUNTAIN VIEW GARDEN

Monterrey, Mexico

Slated for completion in 2021
In conjunction with Carranza | Ruiz Arquitectura

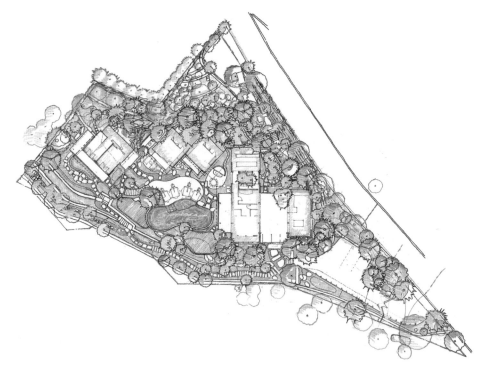

PRIVATE VILLA GARDEN

Saint Barthelemy

Slated for Completion in 2021
In conjunction with Johannes Zingerle of Design Affairs

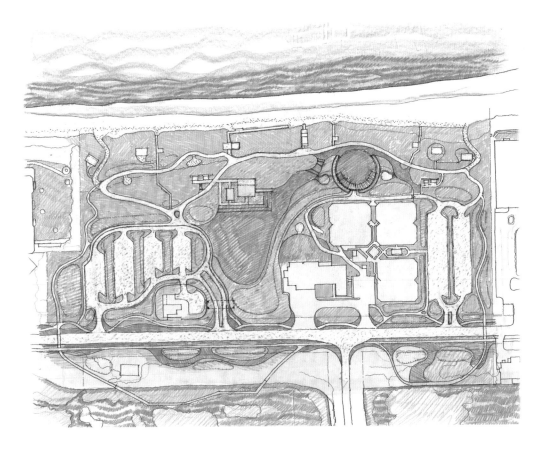

PHIPPS OCEAN PARK
MASTER PLAN

Palm Beach, Florida

In conjunction with the Preservation Foundation
of Palm Beach and the Town of Palm Beach

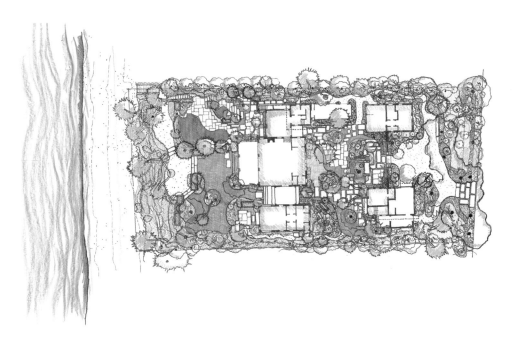

BAKER'S BAY GARDEN

Great Guana Cay, The Bahamas

Completed in 2020; currently being restored after Hurrican Damian.
In conjunction with Raul Lastra of Discovery Design Bahamas

HONORS AND AWARDS

2020

Award of Merit | New York Chapter, ASLA | The Modernist Garden, New York Botanical Garden

Interiors Honor Award | New York Chapter, AIA | Atrium Garden, Ford Foundation Center for Social Justice

Award of Honor | Florida Chapter, ASLA | Coccoloba Garden

2019

Award of Honor | New York Chapter, ASLA | Atrium Garden, Ford Foundation Center for Social Justice

Award of Honor | Florida Chapter, ASLA | Atrium Garden, Ford Foundation Center for Social Justice

Award of Merit | Florida Chapter, ASLA | Faena House Garden

Award of Merit | Florida Chapter, ASLA | Grove Studio Garden

2018

Award of Honor | Florida Chapter, ASLA | Grove at Grand Bay Garden

Award of Honor | Florida Chapter, ASLA | Pine Tree North Garden

2017

Award of Excellence | Florida Chapter, ASLA | Leon Levy Native Plant Preserve

Award of Honor | Florida Chapter, ASLA | Masía Eolo

Garden of Excellence | American Public Gardens Association | Naples Botanical Garden

Private Gardens Typology Award | Architizer A+ Award | Pine Tree North Garden

Florida-Friendly Landscape Award | Florida Nursery, Growers and Landscape Association | Pine Tree North Garden

2016

Frederic B. Stresau Award of Excellence | Florida Chapter, ASLA | El Alear Garden

Award of Excellence | Florida Chapter, ASLA | El Alear Garden

Environmental Sustainability Award | Florida Chapter, ASLA | El Alear Garden

Award of Merit | Florida Chapter, ASLA | Soho Beach House Garden

Award of Honor | Florida Chapter, ASLA | Big Timber Garden

2020 (continued)

Award of Honor | Florida Chapter, ASLA | Visitor Center Garden, Naples Botanical Garden

Architecture and Water Typology Award | Architizer A+ Award | Casa Bahia Garden

2015

Frederic B. Stresau Award of Excellence | Florida Chapter, ASLA | Ventana de la Montaña

Award of Excellence | Florida Chapter, ASLA | Ventana de la Montaña

Award of Honor | Florida Chapter, ASLA | Miami Beach Botanical Garden

Award of Excellence | Florida Nursery, Growers and Landscape Association | Orion Jet Center

2014

Award of Honor | National ASLA | Sky Garden

Award of Merit | Florida Chapter, ASLA | Pavilion Beach Club

2013

Award of Honor | Florida Chapter, ASLA | Sky Garden

Award of Honor| Florida Chapter, ASLA | Golden Rock Inn

Landscapes and Gardens Typology Award | Architizer A+ Award | 1111 Lincoln Road

2012

Award of Excellence in Landscape Architecture | Miami Chapter, AIA | 1111 Lincoln Road

Award of Honor | Florida Chapter, ASLA | Miami Beach Modern Garden

Award of Honor | Jacksonville Chapter, AIA | Refugio do Gatao Garden

2011

City of Miami Beach Beautification Award | 1111 Lincoln Road

City of Miami Beach Certificate of Appreciation | Miami Beach Botanical Garden

Award of Excellence | Florida Chapter, ASLA | 1111 Lincoln Road

Award of Honor | Florida Chapter, ASLA | Brazilian Garden, Naples Botanical Garden

Award of Honor | Florida Chapter, ASLA | Coconut Grove, FL Garden

2010

Award of Excellence | Florida Nursery, Growers and Landscape
  Association | Brazilian Garden, Naples Botanical Garden
Award of Excellence | Florida Chapter, ASLA | Brazilian Modern
  Orchid Show
Award of Merit | Florida Chapter, ASLA | The Davids Garden

2009

Award of Excellence | Florida Nursery, Growers and Landscape
  Association | Gretchen's Garden
Environmental Improvement Grand Award | The Professional
  Landcare Network | River Hammock House

2008

Frederic B. Stresau Award of Excellence | Florida Chapter, ASLA |
  Stone Reef House Garden
Award of Excellence | Florida Chapter, ASLA | Stone Reef House
  Garden
Award of Honor | Florida Chapter, ASLA | Grovenor Rooftop Garden
Award of Merit | Florida Chapter, ASLA | Anagrethel & Samuel
  Lewis Garden
Power Players |Florida International Magazine | People of Like
  Mind
Stars of Design Award | Design Center of the Americas |
  Landscape Design

2007

Award of Honor | Florida Chapter, ASLA | Cornfeld Garden
Design Awards Juror | National ASLA

2006

Elected Fellow of the American Society of Landscape Architects

2005

Award of Honor | National ASLA | Island Modern
Frederic B. Stresau Award of Excellence | Florida Chapter, ASLA |
  Island Modern
Award of Excellence | Florida Chapter, ASLA | Island Modern
Award of Honor | Florida Chapter, ASLA | Casa Morada

2004

Award of Excellence | Florida Chapter, ASLA | Hyatt Windward
  Point Resort
Award of Merit | Florida Chapter, ASLA | Bergeron Garden

2003

Landscape Architect of the Year | Miami Chapter, AIA

2002

Award of Merit | Florida Chapter, ASLA | Montifiore Garden
Award of Merit | Florida Chapter, ASLA | Spanish Tropical Garden

2001

Frederic B. Stresau Award of Excellence | Florida Chapter, ASLA |
  Dunn Garden
Award of Excellence | Florida Chapter, ASLA | Dunn Garden
Award of Excellence | Florida Chapter, ASLA | Swerdlow Garden
Award of Recognition | Florida Chapter, ASLA | Lectures

2000

Named Distinguished Alumnus | University of Florida

1998

Award of Excellence | Florida Chapter, ASLA | Salinero Garden
Award of Merit | Florida Chapter, ASLA | Marquesa Hotel

1997

Frederic B. Stresau Award of Excellence | Florida Chapter, ASLA |
  Hyatt Sunset Harbor Resort
Award of Excellence | Florida Chapter, ASLA | Hyatt Sunset Harbor
  Resort
Award of Excellence | Florida Chapter, ASLA | Coconut Beach
  Resort Hotel
Award of Merit | Florida Chapter, ASLA | Paradise Inn

1996

Award of Excellence | Florida Chapter, ASLA | Coral Gables Garden
Award of Excellence | Florida Chapter, ASLA | Sims Garden

1995

Award of Excellence | Florida Chapter, ASLA | Landes Garden
Award of Honor | Florida Chapter, ASLA | Neukomm Garden
Award of Honor | Florida Chapter, ASLA | Worrell Enterprises
Environmental Improvement Grand Award | American Landscape
  Contractor's Association | Ocean Reef Club
Award of Excellence | Florida Nursery, Growers and Landscape
  Association | Ocean Reef Club

1992

Gold Award | American Resort Development Association | Coconut
  Beach Resort Hotel

ACKNOWLEDGMENTS

RAYMOND JUNGLES

Joy is what my life brings me. I am passionate about designing gardens that bring humans closer to nature. I am dedicated to being the best landscape architect I can be.

Creating habitat for local flora and fauna as well as humans in our gardens is a daily pleasure. Plants and animals have always enticed me, and opportunities to learn more about them present themselves to me in my work.

Beauty surrounds me both in my home as well as in my studio. My lovely and creative wife, Gina DeSouza Jungles, is my design partner in both environments. We live and work in habitats that demonstrate our ideals.

We surround ourselves with likeminded individuals—clients and teammates who provide opportunities, support, and creative ideas. I am grateful to all of those with whom I have had the pleasure to work with—talented RJI team members, architects, interior designers, engineers, builders, contractors, consultants, craftsmen and women, nurserymen and women, and tree brokers all play a vital role.

It takes great concentrated energy and purpose to bring to life a particular vision. For family, this involves passionate participation and sacrifice. Thank you Gina, Benjamin, and Amanda Jungles, and my stepdaughter, Nicole Cohen, a talented writer. Benjamin Burle Jungles is an authority on Florida's native plants and designs his gardens to highlight them.

To my idol, Michael Van Valkenburgh, whose work I have followed and admired since I discovered it while in college, I thank you for agreeing to write the introduction to this book. I was thrilled when you said yes.

I want to acknowledge Phaidon, Monacelli Press, Gianfranco Monacelli, Elizabeth White, and Phil Kovacevich who contributed to the success of this physical creation. Elizabeth refined our project narratives and worked with Amanda and Phil in articulating a brilliant layout to complement the earlier monographs published by Monacelli. To the many photographers who brilliantly captured these gardens, my deepest gratitude.

I dedicate this book to my daughter, Amanda Eva Jungles. Her many talents and commitment to our brand are invaluable. This is the second monograph she has single-handedly curated. You are a joy!

Illustration Credits

Marion Brenner 2–3, 6, 7, 241
Steven Brooke 4–5, 10, 109, 111, 112–113, 114, 168, 172, 173, 174–75, 176–77, 178–79
Barrett Doherty 19 bottom right, 24, 25, 26, 143, 144, 147, 148–49, 153
Bryce Donner 52 top
Stephen Dunn Back cover, 1, 6, 7, 10, 14, 16, 20, 27, 28–29, 61, 64, 68–69, 71, 72–73, 74, 76–77, 78, 81, 82–83, 84–85, 86–87, 88–89, 90–91, 92–93, 100–101, 102, 105, 106, 110, 115, 116, 120–121, 122, 123, 124–25, 126, 127, 128–29, 150–51, 152, 154, 156 bottom, 157, 158–59, 160, 161, 162, 163, 164–65, 166–67, 188, 192 bottom, 193, 194–95, 196–97, 204, 207, 218, 238, 242, 243, 244–45
Joe Fletcher 228
Roger Foley 30, 35, 38–39, 46 top
Robin Hill Cover, 6, 8, 11, 12, 40, 44–45,46 bottom, 47, 48, 52 bottom, 53, 54–55, 56–57, 58–59, 60, 62–63, 67, 70, 75, 198, 200–01, 202, 203, 208–9, 210–11, 212, 214–15, 216, 217, 218, 219, 220, 223, 224–25, 226, 227, 231, 232, 233, 234, 235, 236, 237
Raymond Jungles 10, 15, 192 top
Adrian Llaguno 130, 133, 134, 135, 136–37, 138–39
Claudio Manzoni 180, 183, 184–85, 186–87
New York Botanical Garden 21
Fran Parente 94, 98–99, 103, 104
Lanny Provo 10
Garrett Rowland 140, 145, 146
Jose Silva 33, 43
Lara Swimmer 34, 36–37
Curtice Taylor 22–23
Douglas Thompson 19 top right, 248 top right, 249 bottom right

Library of Congress Control Number 2021935191

ISBN 978-158093-582-1

Design: Phil Kovacevich
Printed in China

The Monacelli Press
65 Bleecker Street
New York, New York 10012